Baked for you with love from:

....

D0420089

Try these tasty:
....
....
Date made:
....
Ingredients:
....
....

Baked for you with love from:

....

Try these tasty:
....
....

Date made:
....

Ingredients:
....
....

Baked for you with love from:

....

Try these tasty:
....
....

Date made:
....

Ingredients:
....
....

Baked for you with love from:

....

Try these tasty:
....
....
Date made:
....
Ingredients:
....
....

Yummy!

Try these tasty...
Baked by...

Yummy!

Try these tasty...
Baked by...

Yummy!

Try these tasty...
Baked by...

Yummy!

Try these tasty...
Baked by...

Yummy!

Try these tasty...
Baked by...

Yummy!

Try these tasty...
Baked by...

Yummy!

Try these tasty...
Baked by...

Yummy!

Try these tasty...
Baked by...

Yummy !

Try these tasty...
Baked by...

Yummy !

Try these tasty...
Baked by...

Yummy !

Try these tasty...
Baked by...

Yummy !

Try these tasty...
Baked by...

Yummy !

Try these tasty...
Baked by...

Yummy !

Try these tasty...
Baked by...

Yummy !

Try these tasty...
Baked by...

Yummy !

Try these tasty...
Baked by...

Home Baking

Home Baking
80 recipes for delicious home-baked goodies

This edition published in 2012
LOVE FOOD is an imprint of Parragon Books Ltd

Parragon
Queen Street House
4 Queen Street
Bath BA1 1HE, UK

Copyright © Parragon Books Ltd 2011

LOVE FOOD and the accompanying heart device is a registered trade mark of Parragon
Books Ltd in Australia, the UK, USA, India and the EU.

www.parragon.com

ISBN: 978-1-4454-2878-9

Printed in China

Cover design by Talking Design
Introduction by Fiona Biggs

Notes for the Reader
This book uses both metric and imperial measurements. Follow the same units of
measurement throughout; do not mix metric and imperial. All spoon measurements are
level: teaspoons are assumed to be 5 ml, and tablespoons are assumed to be 15 ml. Unless
otherwise stated, milk is assumed to be full fat, eggs and individual vegetables are medium,
and pepper is freshly ground black pepper.

The times given are an approximate guide only. Preparation times differ according to the
techniques used by different people and the cooking times may also vary from those
given. Optional ingredients, variations or serving suggestions have not been included in the
calculations.

Recipes using raw or very lightly cooked eggs should be avoided by infants, the elderly,
pregnant women, convalescents and anyone suffering from an illness. Pregnant and
breastfeeding women are advised to avoid eating peanuts and peanut products. Sufferers
from nut allergies should be aware that some of the ready-made ingredients used in the
recipes in this book may contain nuts. Always check the packaging before use.

CONTENTS

INTRODUCTION

Home baking is one of the ultimate feel-good activities, is surprisingly creative and satisfying, and is a great way to impress your friends and show your family how much you care. It's hard to beat the tantalizing aroma of cookies, cakes and pies as you take them out of the oven. Because they contain no preservatives, artificial flavourings or hydrogenated fats, you know they're better in every way than the shop-bought variety.

Baking is also a great way to get children involved in cooking with you – little ones just love stirring cake mixture, rolling out dough and decorating the finished products.

Cakes and cookies make great gifts, whether you've been invited for a meal, or for a special family or festive occasion, or even if you're just dropping in. You can make your creations look even more special by packaging them beautifully and attaching one of the gift labels in the front of this book. Simply cut out a label, fill in the details and attach it to the packing with a length of pretty ribbon. Home-made cakes, pies and cookies are always in demand at garden fêtes and cake sales – again, the packaging will enhance the presentation. If you're supplying a cake or large pie, it will really stand out if you attach one of the cake flags in the front of the book. To assemble, cut out the flag and fold along the dotted line, then place a cocktail stick along the fold and glue together the two halves to secure.

The Basics

Once you're familiar with the ground rules baking is not difficult to master – as soon as you've had a few successes, you'll find it hard to stop!

- First, read the recipe carefully, gather together and weigh all the ingredients you will need.
- Do any chopping, slicing or grating of the ingredients before you start mixing.
- Preheat the oven to the required heat. You can check the temperature using a special oven thermometer
- Bring cake ingredients up to room temperature before using.
- When making pastry, butter or margarine should be kept in the refrigerator until it is needed.
- Don't take shortcuts – allow for chilling and cooling, if required, and factor this into your preparation time.
- When it comes to cake tins, size really does matter. Use the size and shape of

cake tin specified in the recipe – using an incorrect tin will produce poor results.

- Follow the instructions for cooling after removal from the oven – many cookies need to cool on the baking sheet and heavier cakes should be left to cool completely in the tin.
- Always store cookies and cakes in separate airtight containers. If stored together cookies will absorb the moisture from cakes.

Equipment

You will need some basic equipment for most baking projects:

- Kitchen scales and/or measuring jugs and spoons
- Wooden spoons in different sizes
- A rolling pin
- A sieve
- A set of mixing bowls and basins, in glass or stainless steel
- A saucepan for melting butter or chocolate (although you can also do this in a bowl in the microwave oven)
- A balloon whisk (an electric mixer is useful, but not essential)
- 1–2 heavy baking sheets
- Cake tins in different shapes and sizes, including some loose-based and springform tins
- Tart tins and loaf tins in different sizes
- Muffin and bun tins
- Cookie cutters in different shapes and sizes
- A rubber spatula
- A pastry brush
- A palette knife
- A wire rack

Top Baking Tips

Armed with a few tricks of the trade, you'll find that baking perfection is easier to achieve than you may think.

- When making cakes, always sift flour before use, even if the flour comes ready-sifted.
- To retain as much air as possible in cake mixtures, fold in flour, sugar and egg whites using a metal spoon or a spatula, and avoid mixing too vigorously.
- To prevent dried fruit, seeds or nuts sinking to the bottom of the cake always add them to the dry cake mixture.
- Grease or line cake tins if this is indicated in the method, even if using non-stick tins. This will prevent burning of the sides and base of the cake.
- Don't be tempted to open the oven door while a cake is baking. The sudden change in temperature may cause your cake to sink in the middle.
- Test whether a cake is cooked by inserting a skewer into the centre – the cake is cooked if the skewer comes out clean. Alternatively, press down lightly on the centre of the cake – it will bounce back if it is cooked.
- Keep pastry as cool as possible during preparation and chill for 30 minutes, wrapped in clingfilm, before baking.
- Your pastry will be lighter if you lift your hands high out of the mixture when rubbing in the fat.
- When melting chocolate over simmering water, always keep the bowl containing the chocolate clear of the water and do not allow any water to splash on the chocolate or it will seize.

Cakes & Pies

Madeira Cake

Serves 8–10

175 g/6 oz unsalted butter,
plus extra for greasing

175 g/6 oz caster sugar

finely grated rind of 1 lemon

3 large eggs, beaten

115 g/4 oz plain flour

115 g/4 oz self-raising flour

2–3 tbsp brandy or milk

2 slices of citron peel

Preheat the oven to 160°C/325°F/Gas Mark 3. Grease and line an 18-cm/7-inch round deep cake tin.

Cream together the butter and sugar until pale and fluffy. Add the lemon rind and gradually beat in the eggs. Sift in the flours and fold in evenly, adding enough brandy to make a soft dropping consistency.

Spoon the mixture into the prepared tin and smooth level. Lay the slices of citron peel on top of the cake.

Bake in the preheated oven for 1–1¼ hours, or until well risen, golden brown and springy to the touch.

Cool in the tin for 10 minutes, then turn out and cool completely on a wire rack.

variation
omit the citron peel, brush the cooked cake with honey and top with glacé fruit

Victoria Sponge Cake

Serves 8–10

175 g/6 oz unsalted butter,
   softened, plus extra for greasing
175 g/6 oz caster sugar
3 eggs, beaten
175 g/6 oz self-raising flour
pinch of salt
3 tbsp raspberry jam
1 tbsp icing sugar

Preheat the oven to 180°C/350°F/Gas Mark 4. Grease and line the bases of two 20-cm/8-inch sandwich tins.

Cream together the butter and caster sugar until pale and fluffy. Gradually add the eggs, beating well after each addition. Sift the flour and salt into the mixture and fold in evenly with a metal spoon.

Divide the mixture between the prepared tins and smooth level. Bake in the preheated oven for 25–30 minutes, until well risen, golden brown and beginning to shrink away from the sides of the tins.

Remove from the oven and leave to stand for 1 minute. Loosen the cakes from around the edge of the tins, then turn out and cool completely on a wire rack.

When completely cool, sandwich the cakes together with the jam and dust with the icing sugar.

Cinnamon Swirl Bundt Cake

Serves 8–10

175 g/6 oz unsalted butter,
  plus extra for greasing
300 g/10½ oz caster sugar
3 eggs, beaten
225 ml/8 fl oz soured cream
1 tsp vanilla extract
280 g/10 oz plain flour,
  plus extra for dusting
1 tsp baking powder
1 tsp bicarbonate of soda
½ tsp salt
55 g/2 oz walnuts, chopped
  (optional)

Swirl

1 tbsp ground cinnamon
3 tbsp soft light brown sugar
2 tbsp granulated sugar

Glaze

115 g/4 oz icing sugar
about 1½ tbsp milk
1 tsp ground cinnamon, or
  to taste

Preheat the oven to 180°C/350°F/Gas Mark 4. Grease a 25-cm/10-inch Bundt cake tin and dust with flour.

Cream together the butter and caster sugar until pale and fluffy. Gradually add in the eggs, beating well after each addition. Beat in the soured cream and vanilla extract until well mixed. Sift in the flour, baking powder, bicarbonate of soda and salt, then mix until just combined. Stir in the walnuts, if using.

Pour half the mixture into the prepared tin and spread evenly. Mix together all the ingredients for the swirl in a small bowl. Sprinkle the swirl evenly around the centre of the cake mixture, then cover with the remaining cake mixture.

Bake in the preheated oven for 50 minutes, until a skewer inserted into the centre of the cake comes out clean. Leave to cool in the tin for 20 minutes before turning out.

For the glaze, sift the icing sugar into a small bowl and stir in enough of the milk to make a thick glaze with a pouring consistency. Stir in the cinnamon, then drizzle the glaze over the top of the cake. Leave to set.

Devil's Food Cake

Serves 8–10

140 g/5 oz plain chocolate,
   broken into pieces
100 ml/3½ fl oz milk
2 tbsp cocoa powder
140 g/5 oz unsalted butter,
   plus extra for greasing
140 g/5 oz light muscovado sugar
3 eggs, separated
4 tbsp soured cream or crème
   fraîche
200 g/7 oz plain flour
1 tsp bicarbonate of soda

Frosting

140 g/5 oz plain chocolate,
   broken into pieces
40 g/1½ oz cocoa powder
4 tbsp soured cream or
   crème fraîche
1 tbsp golden syrup
40 g/1½ oz unsalted butter
4 tbsp water
200 g/7 oz icing sugar

Preheat the oven to 160°C/325°F/ Gas Mark 3. Grease and line the bases of two 20-cm/8-inch sandwich tins. Place the chocolate, milk and cocoa powder in a heatproof bowl over a saucepan of hot water, then heat gently, stirring, until melted and smooth.

Cream together the butter and muscovado sugar until pale and fluffy. Beat in the egg yolks, then the soured cream and the chocolate mixture. Sift in the flour and bicarbonate of soda, then fold in evenly. In a separate bowl, whisk the egg whites until holding firm peaks. Fold into the mixture lightly and evenly.

Divide the mixture between the prepared tins. Bake in the preheated oven for 35–40 minutes, or until risen and firm to the touch. Cool in the tins for 10 minutes, then turn out onto a wire rack.

For the frosting, place the chocolate, cocoa powder, soured cream, golden syrup, butter and water in a saucepan and heat gently until melted. Remove from the heat and sift in the icing sugar, stirring until smooth. Leave to cool until the mixture begins to thicken. Split the cakes in half to make four layers, then sandwich together with a third of the frosting. Spread the remaining frosting over the top and sides of the cake.

Classic Cherry Cake

Serves 8

250 g/9 oz glacé cherries, quartered

85 g/3 oz ground almonds

200 g/7 oz plain flour

1 tsp baking powder

200 g/7 oz unsalted butter, plus extra for greasing

200 g/7 oz caster sugar

3 large eggs

juice and finely grated rind of 1 lemon

6 sugar cubes, crushed

Preheat the oven to 180°C/350°F/Gas Mark 4. Grease and line a 20-cm/8-inch round cake tin.

Stir together the glacé cherries, ground almonds and 1 tablespoon of the flour. Sift the remaining flour into a separate bowl with the baking powder.

Cream together the butter and sugar until pale and fluffy. Gradually add the eggs, beating well after each addition.

Add the flour mixture and fold lightly and evenly into the creamed mixture with a metal spoon. Add the cherry mixture and fold in evenly. Finally, fold in the lemon juice and rind.

Spoon the mixture into the prepared tin and sprinkle with the crushed sugar cubes. Bake in the preheated oven for 1–1¼ hours, or until risen, golden brown and beginning to shrink away from the sides of the tin.

Cool in the tin for about 15 minutes, then turn out and cool completely on a wire rack.

Coffee &
Walnut Cake

Serves 8

175 g/6 oz unsalted butter,
    plus extra for greasing
175 g/6 oz light muscovado sugar
3 large eggs, beaten
3 tbsp strong black coffee
175 g/6 oz self-raising flour
1½ tsp baking powder
115 g/4 oz walnuts, chopped
walnut halves, to decorate

Frosting

115 g/4 oz unsalted butter
200 g/7 oz icing sugar
1 tbsp strong black coffee
½ tsp vanilla extract

Preheat the oven to 180°C/350°F/Gas Mark 4. Grease and line the bases of two 20-cm/8-inch sandwich tins.

Cream together the butter and muscovado sugar until pale and fluffy. Gradually add the eggs, beating well after each addition. Beat in the coffee.

Sift the flour and baking powder into the mixture, then fold in lightly and evenly with a metal spoon. Fold in the chopped walnuts.

Divide the mixture between the prepared tins and smooth level. Bake in the preheated oven for 20–25 minutes, or until golden brown and springy to the touch. Turn out onto a wire rack to cool.

For the frosting, beat together the butter, icing sugar, coffee and vanilla extract, mixing until smooth and creamy.

Use about half the frosting to sandwich the cakes together, then spread the remaining frosting on top and swirl with a palette knife. Decorate with walnut halves.

Country Fruit Cake

Serves 10

175 g/6 oz plain white flour

70 g/2½ oz plain wholemeal flour

2 tsp baking powder

½ tsp ground nutmeg

175 g/6 oz unsalted butter,
softened, plus extra for greasing

175 g/6 oz light muscovado sugar

3 eggs, beaten

1 tsp vanilla extract

1 tbsp milk

200 g/7 oz mixed dried fruit

1 tbsp demerara sugar

Preheat the oven to 160°C/325°F/Gas Mark 3. Grease and line a 20-cm/8-inch round deep cake tin.

Sift the flours, baking powder and nutmeg into a large bowl, adding any bran left in the sieve. Add the butter, muscovado sugar, eggs and vanilla extract. Beat well until the mixture is smooth, then stir in the milk and mixed dried fruit.

Spoon the mixture into the prepared tin and smooth level with a palette knife. Sprinkle the demerara sugar evenly over the surface. Bake in the preheated oven for 1 hour 20 minutes–1 hour 30 minutes, or until risen, firm and golden brown.

Leave to cool in the tin for about 20 minutes, then turn out and cool completely on a wire rack.

great tip!
stop the dried fruit from sinking by tossing with a little flour before using

Carrot Cake with Cream Cheese Frosting

Serves 8 ·

225 g/8 oz plain flour

1 tsp salt

2 tsp baking powder

1 tsp bicarbonate of soda

2 tsp ground cinnamon

½ tsp ground ginger

400 g/14 oz caster sugar

300 ml/10 fl oz vegetable oil

4 eggs

55 g/2 oz unsalted butter, melted,
    plus extra for greasing

280 g/10 oz carrots, grated

225 g/8 oz canned crushed
    pineapple, drained

55 g/2 oz pecan nuts, chopped

55 g/2 oz walnuts, chopped

shop-bought carrot decorations,
    to decorate

Frosting

115 g/4 oz unsalted butter,
    softened

225 g/8 oz cream cheese,
    softened

1 tbsp milk

1 tsp vanilla extract

450 g/1 lb icing sugar

Preheat the oven to 180°C/350°F/Gas Mark 4. Lightly grease a 33 x 23-cm/ 13 x 9-inch baking dish.

Sift together the flour, salt, baking powder, bicarbonate of soda, cinnamon and ginger into a bowl and set aside.

Whisk together the caster sugar, oil and eggs in a separate bowl until thoroughly combined. Whisk in the melted butter. Stir in the carrots, pineapple and nuts with a spatula, then stir in the flour mixture in two batches.

Spoon the mixture into the prepared dish. Bake in the preheated oven for 40 minutes, until risen and firm to the touch. Leave to cool completely in the dish before frosting.

For the frosting, using an electric mixer, beat together the butter, cream cheese, milk and vanilla extract until light and fluffy. Gradually beat in the icing sugar until smooth. Spread the frosting evenly over the cooled cake and top each portion with a carrot decoration.

Banana Nut Bread

Serves 6–8

225 g/8 oz plain flour, plus
    extra for dusting

1 tsp salt

1 tsp baking powder

1 tsp bicarbonate of soda

115 g/4 oz unsalted butter,
    softened, plus extra for greasing

200 g/7 oz caster sugar

2 eggs

3 bananas, mashed

115 g/4 oz walnuts, chopped

2 tbsp milk

Preheat the oven to 160°C/325°F/Gas
Mark 3. Grease and lightly flour a 900-g/
2-lb loaf tin.

Sift together the flour, salt, baking powder
and bicarbonate of soda into a bowl and
set aside.

Cream together the butter and sugar in a
separate bowl until pale and fluffy. Gradually
add the eggs, beating well after each
addition. Stir in the bananas, walnuts and
milk until thoroughly mixed. Add the flour
mixture, stirring until just combined.

Spoon the mixture into the prepared tin.
Bake in the preheated oven for 1 hour
10 minutes, until a skewer inserted into
the centre comes out clean. Leave to cool
in the tin for 20 minutes before turning out.

variation
use pecan nuts instead of
walnuts

Caribbean Coconut Cake

Serves 10

280 g/10 oz unsalted butter,
    softened, plus extra for greasing
175 g/6 oz golden caster sugar
3 eggs
175 g/6 oz self-raising flour
1½ tsp baking powder
½ tsp freshly grated nutmeg
55 g/2 oz desiccated coconut
5 tbsp coconut cream
280 g/10 oz icing sugar
5 tbsp pineapple jam
toasted desiccated coconut,
    to decorate

Preheat the oven to 180°C/350°F/Gas Mark 4. Grease and line the bases of two 20-cm/8-inch sandwich tins.

Place 175 g/6 oz of the butter in a bowl with the caster sugar and eggs and sift in the flour, baking powder and nutmeg. Beat together until smooth, then stir in the desiccated coconut and 2 tablespoons of the coconut cream.

Divide the mixture between the prepared tins and smooth level. Bake in the preheated oven for 25 minutes, or until golden and firm to the touch. Leave to cool in the tins for 5 minutes, then turn out and cool completely on a wire rack.

Sift the icing sugar into a bowl and add the remaining butter and coconut cream. Beat together until smooth. Spread the jam over one of the cakes and top with just under half of the buttercream. Place the second cake on top. Spread the remaining buttercream on top of the cake and scatter with toasted desiccated coconut.

Red Velvet Cake

Serves 12

225 g/8 oz unsalted butter,
plus extra for greasing
4 tbsp water
55 g/2 oz cocoa powder
3 eggs
250 ml/9 fl oz buttermilk
2 tsp vanilla extract
2 tbsp red food colouring
280 g/10 oz plain flour
55 g/2 oz cornflour
1½ tsp baking powder
280 g/10 oz caster sugar

Frosting

250 g/9 oz full-fat soft cheese
40 g/1½ oz unsalted butter
3 tbsp caster sugar
1 tsp vanilla extract

Preheat the oven to 190°C/375°F/Gas Mark 5. Grease and line the bases of two 23-cm/9-inch sandwich tins.

Place the butter, water and cocoa powder in a small saucepan and heat gently, without boiling, stirring until melted and smooth. Remove from the heat and leave to cool slightly.

Beat together the eggs, buttermilk, vanilla extract and food colouring until frothy. Beat in the butter mixture. Sift together the flour, cornflour and baking powder, then stir into the mixture with the sugar.

Divide the mixture between the prepared tins and bake in the preheated oven for 25–30 minutes, or until risen and firm to the touch. Leave to cool in the tins for 3–4 minutes, then turn out and cool completely on a wire rack.

For the frosting, beat together all the ingredients until smooth. Use about half of the frosting to sandwich the cakes together, then spread the remainder over the top, swirling with a palette knife.

Date &
Walnut Teabread

Serves 8
100 g/3½ oz stoned dates, chopped
½ tsp bicarbonate of soda
finely grated rind of ½ lemon
100 ml/3½ fl oz hot tea
40 g/1½ oz unsalted butter, plus extra for greasing
70 g/2½ oz light muscovado sugar
1 small egg
125 g/4½ oz self-raising flour
25 g/1 oz walnuts, chopped
walnut halves, to decorate

Preheat the oven to 180°C/350°F/Gas Mark 4. Grease and line the base of a 450-g/1-lb loaf tin.

Place the dates, bicarbonate of soda and lemon rind in a bowl and add the hot tea. Leave to soak for 10 minutes, until soft.

Cream together the butter and sugar until light and fluffy, then beat in the egg. Stir in the date mixture.

Fold in the flour using a large metal spoon, then fold in the chopped walnuts. Spoon the mixture into the prepared tin and smooth level. Top with walnut halves.

Bake in the preheated oven for 35–40 minutes, or until risen, firm and golden brown. Cool for 10 minutes in the tin, then turn out cool completely on a wire rack.

great tip!
to serve, cut the teabread into slices and butter thickly

Sticky Ginger Loaf

Serves 8–10

butter, for greasing

175 g/6 oz plain flour

1 tbsp baking powder

1 tbsp ground ginger

175 ml/6 fl oz sunflower oil

85 g/3 oz dark muscovado sugar

85 g/3 oz golden syrup

3 eggs, beaten

3 pieces stem ginger in syrup, drained and finely chopped, plus 2 tbsp syrup from the jar

sliced stem ginger, to decorate

Preheat the oven to 180°C/350°F/Gas Mark 4. Grease and line a 1.2-litre/2-pint loaf tin.

Sift the flour, baking powder and ground ginger into a large bowl. Add the oil, sugar, golden syrup and eggs, then beat well to a smooth batter. Stir in the chopped ginger.

Pour the mixture into the prepared tin. Bake in the preheated oven for 1–1¼ hours, until well risen and firm to the touch.

Leave to cool in the tin for 10 minutes, then turn out and finish cooling on a wire rack. To serve, brush the top of the cake with the ginger syrup, decorate with sliced ginger and cut into slices.

great tip!
this cake will taste even better if kept in an airtight container for a day before eating

Apple Pie

Serves 6

Pastry

350 g/12 oz plain flour

pinch of salt

85 g/3 oz cold unsalted butter or margarine, cut into small pieces

85 g/3 oz cold lard or white vegetable fat, cut into small pieces

1–2 tbsp cold water

beaten egg or milk, for glazing

Filling

750 g–1 kg/1 lb 10 oz–2 lb 4 oz cooking apples, peeled, cored and sliced

125 g/4½ oz soft light brown sugar or caster sugar, plus extra for sprinkling

½–1 tsp ground cinnamon, mixed spice or ground ginger

1–2 tbsp water (optional)

To make the pastry, sift the flour and salt into a large bowl. Rub in the butter and lard until the mixture resembles breadcrumbs. Add the water and mix to a dough. Wrap in clingfilm and chill for 30 minutes.

Preheat the oven to 220°C/425°F/Gas Mark 7. Roll out almost two thirds of the pastry thinly and use to line a deep 23-cm/9-inch pie plate or pie tin.

Mix the apples with the sugar and spice and pack into the pastry case. Add the water if needed, particularly if the apples are not very juicy.

Roll out the remaining pastry to form a lid. Dampen the edges of the pie rim with water and position the lid, pressing the edges firmly together. Trim and crimp the edges.

Using the trimmings, cut out leaves or other shapes to decorate the top of the pie. Dampen and attach. Glaze the top of the pie with beaten egg or milk, make a small hole in the top and place the pie on a baking sheet.

Bake in the preheated oven for 20 minutes, then reduce the oven temperature to 180°C/350°F/Gas Mark 4 and bake for a further 30 minutes, or until the pastry is a light golden brown. Serve hot or cold, sprinkled with sugar.

Latticed Cherry Pie

Serves 8

140 g/5 oz plain flour
¼ tsp baking powder
½ tsp ground mixed spice
½ tsp salt
50 g/1¾ oz caster sugar
55 g/2 oz cold unsalted butter, diced, plus extra for greasing
1 egg, beaten, plus extra for glazing

Filling

900 g/2 lb stoned fresh cherries, or canned cherries, drained
150 g/5½ oz caster sugar
½ tsp almond extract
2 tsp cherry brandy
¼ tsp ground mixed spice
2 tbsp cornflour
2 tbsp water
25 g/1 oz unsalted butter

To make the pastry, sift the flour, baking powder, mixed spice and salt into a large bowl. Stir in the sugar. Rub in the butter until the mixture resembles breadcrumbs. Add the egg and mix to a dough. Wrap in clingfilm and chill for 30 minutes.

Preheat the oven to 220°C/425°F/Gas Mark 7. Grease a 23-cm/9-inch tart tin. Roll out the pastry into two 30-cm/12-inch rounds and use one to line the prepared tin.

Put half the cherries and the sugar into a saucepan. Simmer over a low heat, stirring, for 5 minutes, or until the sugar has melted. Stir in the almond extract, brandy and mixed spice. Mix together the cornflour and water. Remove the pan from the heat and stir in the cornflour paste, then return to the heat and stir constantly until the mixture boils and thickens. Leave to cool slightly. Stir in the remaining cherries, pour into the pastry case, then dot with the butter.

Cut the second pastry round into 11 strips and place over the filling to form a lattice. Trim off the edges, crimp the rim and brush with beaten egg. Cover with foil, then bake in the preheated oven for 30 minutes. Discard the foil, then bake for a further 15 minutes, or until golden.

Key Lime Pie

Serves 6–8

175 g/6 oz digestive biscuits or ginger biscuits

2 tbsp caster sugar

½ tsp ground cinnamon

85 g/3 oz unsalted butter, melted, plus extra for greasing

Filling

400 ml/14 fl oz canned condensed milk

125 ml/4 fl oz lime juice

finely grated rind of 3 limes

4 large egg yolks

Preheat the oven to 160°C/325°F/ Gas Mark 3. Lightly grease a 23-cm/9-inch pie plate, about 4 cm/1½ inches deep.

To make the crumb crust, put the biscuits, sugar and cinnamon into a food processor and process until fine crumbs form — do not overprocess to a powder. Add the melted butter and process again until moistened.

Tip the crumb mixture into the prepared pie plate and press over the base and up the sides. Transfer to a baking sheet and bake in the preheated oven for 5 minutes.

Meanwhile, beat the condensed milk, lime juice, lime rind, reserving some for decoration, and egg yolks together in a bowl until well blended.

Remove the crumb crust from the oven, pour the filling into the crumb crust and spread out to the edges. Bake for a further 15 minutes, or until the filling is set around the edges but still wobbly in the centre. Remove from the oven and leave to cool completely, then cover and chill in the refrigerator for at least 2 hours. Decorate with the reserved lime rind before serving.

Boston Cream Pie

Serves 8
225 g/8 oz self-raising flour
½ tsp salt
1 tsp baking powder
115 g/4 oz unsalted butter,
    softened, plus extra for greasing
200 g/7 oz caster sugar
2 eggs, beaten
175 ml/6 fl oz milk

Pastry cream
100 g/3½oz caster sugar
2 tbsp cornflour
3 eggs
225 ml/8 fl oz double cream
225 ml/8 fl oz milk
15 g/½oz unsalted butter
1½ tsp vanilla extract
pinch of salt

Chocolate topping
115 g/4 oz plain chocolate,
    broken into pieces
125 ml/4 fl oz double cream
1 tsp butter

For the pastry cream, whisk together the sugar, cornflour and eggs until the whisk leaves a ribbon trail when lifted. Set aside. Bring the cream, milk and butter to the boil in a pan. Add the sugar mixture and boil, whisking constantly, for 1 minute, until thickened, then strain into a bowl. Cover the surface with clingfilm and chill overnight.

Preheat the oven to 190°C/375°F/Gas Mark 5. Grease two 20-cm/8-inch sandwich tins. Sift the flour, salt and baking powder into a bowl and set aside. Cream together the butter and sugar until pale and fluffy. Gradually add the eggs, mixing well after each addition. Gradually add the milk, alternating with the flour mixture, and stir to combine. Divide the mixture between the prepared tins. Bake in the preheated oven for 25 minutes, until well risen and firm to the touch. Turn out onto a wire rack to cool.

Put the chocolate into a heatproof bowl. Bring the cream and butter to simmering point in a small saucepan, then pour over the chocolate. Leave to stand for 3 minutes, then whisk gently to mix. Leave to cool and thicken. Whisk the vanilla extract and salt into the pastry cream, then spread it over one of the cakes. Top with the second cake, then spread with the chocolate topping.

New York Cheesecake

Serves 10

150 g/5½ oz digestive biscuits

1 tbsp granulated sugar

100 g/3½ oz unsalted butter, melted, plus extra for greasing

900 g/2 lb cream cheese

250 g/9 oz caster sugar

2 tbsp plain flour

1 tsp vanilla extract

finely grated rind of 1 orange

finely grated rind of 1 lemon

3 eggs

2 egg yolks

300 ml/10 fl oz double cream

Preheat the oven to 180°C/350°F/Gas Mark 4. Grease a 23-cm/9-inch round springform cake tin.

To make the crumb crust, put the biscuits and granulated sugar into food processor and process until fine crumbs form – do not overprocess to a powder. Add the melted butter and process again until moistened. Tip the crumb mixture into the prepared tin and press over the base. Bake in the preheated oven for 10 minutes. Leave to cool on a wire rack.

Increase the oven temperature to 200°C/400°F/Gas Mark 6. Using an electric mixer, beat the cream cheese, then gradually add the caster sugar and flour and beat until smooth. Increase the speed and beat in the vanilla extract, orange rind and lemon rind, then add in the eggs and egg yolks, one at a time. Finally, beat in the cream. The mixture should be light and fluffy.

Pour the cream cheese mixture into the tin and smooth level. Transfer to the oven and bake for 15 minutes, then reduce the temperature to 100°C/200°F/Gas Mark ¼ and bake for a further 30 minutes. Turn off the oven and leave the cheesecake in it for 2 hours to cool and set. Cover and chill overnight.

Mississippi Mud Pie

Serves 12–14

140 g/5 oz digestive biscuits
85 g/3 oz pecan nuts,
    finely chopped
1 tbsp soft light brown sugar
½ tsp ground cinnamon
85 g/3 oz unsalted butter, melted

Filling
225 g/8 oz unsalted butter
    or margarine, plus extra
    for greasing
175 g/6 oz plain chocolate,
    chopped
125 ml/4 fl oz golden syrup
4 large eggs, beaten
85 g/3 oz pecan nuts,
    finely chopped

Preheat the oven to 180°C/350°F/Gas Mark 4. Lightly grease a 23-cm/9-inch round springform cake tin.

To make the crumb crust, put the biscuits, pecan nuts, sugar and cinnamon into a food processor and process until fine crumbs form – do not overprocess to a powder. Add the melted butter and process again until moistened.

Tip the crumb mixture into the prepared tin and press over the base and about 4 cm/1½ inches up the sides of the tin. Cover the tin and chill while you make the filling.

To make the filling, put the butter, chocolate and golden syrup into a saucepan over a low heat and stir until melted and blended. Leave to cool, then beat in the eggs and pecan nuts.

Pour the filling into the tin and smooth level. Bake in the preheated oven for 30 minutes, or until just set but still soft in the centre. Leave to cool on a wire rack. Serve at room temperature or chilled.

Sweet Pumpkin Pie

Serves 6–8

1.8 kg/4 lb sweet pumpkin, halved and deseeded

140 g/5 oz plain flour, plus extra for dusting

¼ tsp baking powder

1½ tsp ground cinnamon

¾ tsp ground nutmeg

¾ tsp ground cloves

1 tsp salt

50 g/1¾ oz caster sugar

55 g/2 oz cold unsalted butter, diced, plus extra for greasing

3 eggs

400 g/14 oz canned condensed milk

½ tsp vanilla extract

1 tbsp demerara sugar

Streusel topping

2 tbsp plain flour

4 tbsp demerara sugar

1 tsp ground cinnamon

25 g/1 oz unsalted butter, diced

75 g/2¾ oz pecan nuts, chopped

75 g/2¾ oz walnuts, chopped

Preheat the oven to 190°C/375°F/Gas Mark 5. Put the pumpkin halves, face down, in a baking tin and cover with foil. Bake in the preheated oven for 1½ hours. Scoop out the flesh and purée in a food processor. Drain off any excess liquid.

Grease a 23-cm/9-inch round tart tin. Sift the flour and baking powder into a bowl. Stir in ½ teaspoon of the cinnamon, ¼ teaspoon of the nutmeg, ¼ teaspoon of the cloves, ½ teaspoon of the salt and the caster sugar. Rub in the butter until the mixture resembles breadcrumbs. Lightly beat one of the eggs, then add to the bowl. Mix together to form a dough, then roll out on a lightly floured surface and use to line the prepared tin. Chill for 30 minutes.

Preheat the oven to 220°C/425°F/Gas Mark 7. Put the pumpkin in a bowl, then stir in the condensed milk and the remaining eggs. Add the remaining spices and salt, then stir in the vanilla extract and demerara sugar. Pour into the pastry case and bake in the preheated oven for 15 minutes.

Mix the flour, demerara sugar and cinnamon in a bowl, rub in the butter, then stir in the nuts. Remove the pie from the oven and reduce the heat to 180°C/350°F/Gas Mark 4. Sprinkle over the topping, then bake for a further 35 minutes. Serve warm.

Sweet Potato Pie

Serves 8

175 g/6 oz plain flour, plus extra
for dusting

½ tsp salt

¼ tsp caster sugar

50 g/1¾ oz cold unsalted butter,
diced

40 g/1½ oz cold white vegetable
fat, diced

2 tbsp cold water

Filling

500 g/1 lb 2 oz orange-fleshed
sweet potatoes, peeled

3 eggs, beaten

100 g/3½ oz soft light brown sugar

350 ml/12 fl oz canned condensed
milk

40 g/1½ oz unsalted butter, melted

2 tsp vanilla extract

1 tsp ground cinnamon

1 tsp ground nutmeg

½ tsp salt

Sift the flour, salt and caster sugar into a bowl. Add the butter and vegetable fat and rub in until the mixture resembles fine breadcrumbs. Add the water and mix to a dough. Wrap in clingfilm and chill for at least 1 hour.

Cook the sweet potatoes in a saucepan of boiling water for 15 minutes. Drain. When cool, mash the potatoes in a bowl and beat in the eggs and brown sugar until very smooth. Beat in the remaining filling ingredients and set aside.

Preheat the oven to 220°C/425°F/Gas Mark 7. Roll out the pastry on a lightly floured surface into a thin 28-cm/11-inch round and use to line a 23-cm/9-inch tart tin, about 4 cm/1½ inches deep. Press a floured fork around the edges and prick the base all over. Line with baking paper, fill with baking beans and bake in the preheated oven for 12 minutes, until light golden. Remove the paper and beans.

Pour the filling into the pastry case and bake for 10 minutes. Reduce the oven temperature to 160°C/325°F/Gas Mark 3 and bake for a further 35 minutes, or until a knife inserted into the centre comes out clean. Leave to cool on a wire rack.

Rhubarb Crumble

Serves 6
900 g/2 lb rhubarb
115 g/4 oz caster sugar
juice and grated rind of 1 orange
cream, yogurt or custard, to serve

Crumble topping
225 g/8 oz plain white or
    wholemeal flour
115 g/4 oz unsalted butter, diced
115 g/4 oz soft light brown sugar
1 tsp ground ginger

Preheat the oven to 190°C/375°F/Gas Mark 5.

Cut the rhubarb into 2.5-cm/1-inch lengths and place in a 1.7-litre/3-pint baking dish with the caster sugar and the orange juice and rind.

To make the crumble topping, sift the flour into a bowl. Rub in the butter with your fingertips until the mixture resembles fine breadcrumbs. Stir in the brown sugar and ginger. Spread evenly over the fruit and press down lightly using a fork.

Place the dish on a baking sheet and bake in the preheated oven for 25–30 minutes, until the crumble is golden brown. Serve warm with cream, yogurt or custard.

variation
for a change, add oats or
nuts to the crumble topping

Bread & Butter Pudding

Serves 4–6
85 g/3 oz unsalted butter, softened
6 slices of thick white bread
55 g/2 oz mixed dried fruit
25 g/1 oz candied peel
3 large eggs
300 ml/10 fl oz milk
150 ml/5 fl oz double cream
55 g/2 oz caster sugar
1 tbsp demerara sugar
freshly grated nutmeg, to taste

Preheat the oven to 180°C/350°F/Gas Mark 4.

Use a little of the butter to grease a 20 x 25-cm/8 x 10-inch baking dish and the remainder to butter the slices of bread. Cut the bread diagonally into quarters and arrange half, overlapping, in the prepared baking dish.

Scatter half the dried fruit and peel over the bread, cover with the remaining bread slices and add the remaining dried fruit and peel.

In a jug, beat the eggs well and mix in the milk, cream and caster sugar. Pour over the pudding and leave to stand for 15 minutes to allow the bread to soak up some of the egg mixture.

Tuck the dried fruit and peel under the bread slices so that they don't burn. Sprinkle over the demerara sugar and nutmeg to taste.

Place the dish on a baking sheet and bake at the top of the oven for 30–40 minutes, until just set and golden brown. Remove from the oven and serve warm.

Cupcakes & Muffins

Vanilla Frosted Cupcakes

Makes 12

115 g/4 oz unsalted butter, softened

115 g/4 oz caster sugar

2 eggs, lightly beaten

115 g/4 oz self-raising flour

1 tbsp milk

1 tbsp hundreds and thousands

Frosting

175 g/6 oz unsalted butter, softened

1 tsp vanilla extract

280 g/10 oz icing sugar

Preheat the oven to 180°C/350°F/Gas Mark 4. Put 12 paper cases in a bun tin.

Cream together the butter and sugar until pale and fluffy. Gradually beat in the eggs. Sift in the flour and, using a metal spoon, fold into the mixture with the milk. Spoon the mixture into the paper cases.

Bake in the preheated oven for 20 minutes, or until golden brown and firm to the touch. Transfer to a wire rack and leave to cool.

To make the frosting, put the butter and vanilla extract in a bowl and, using an electric mixer, beat until the butter is pale and very soft. Gradually sift in the icing sugar, beating well after each addition.

Spoon the frosting into a large piping bag fitted with a medium star-shaped nozzle and pipe large swirls of frosting on the top of each cupcake. Sprinkle with the hundreds and thousands.

Chocolate Hazelnut Cupcakes

Makes 18

175 g/6 oz unsalted butter, softened

115 g/4 oz soft light brown sugar

2 large eggs, lightly beaten

2 tbsp chocolate and hazelnut spread

175 g/6 oz self-raising flour

50 g/1¾ oz blanched hazelnuts, roughly ground

Topping

5 tbsp chocolate and hazelnut spread

18 whole blanched hazelnuts

Preheat the oven to 180°C/350°F/Gas Mark 4. Put 18 paper cases in bun tins.

Cream together the butter and sugar until pale and fluffy. Gradually beat in the eggs, then stir in the chocolate and hazelnut spread. Sift in the flour and, using a metal spoon, fold into the mixture with the ground hazelnuts. Spoon the mixture into the paper cases.

Bake in the preheated oven for 20–25 minutes or until risen and firm to the touch. Transfer to a wire rack and leave to cool.

When the cupcakes are cold, swirl a little of the chocolate and hazelnut spread over the top of each cupcake and top with a hazelnut.

great tip!
make a hollow in the top of the cooked cupcakes and fill with chocolate spread

Blueberry Cupcakes with Soured Cream Frosting

Makes 30

175 g/6 oz plain flour

1 tbsp baking powder

175 g/6 oz unsalted butter, softened

175 g/6 oz caster sugar

3 eggs, beaten

1 tsp vanilla extract

finely grated rind of ½ orange

150 g/5½ oz fresh blueberries

Frosting

3 tbsp soured cream

150 g/5½ oz icing sugar

Preheat the oven to 190°C/375°F/Gas Mark 5. Put 30 paper cases in bun tins.

Sift the flour and baking powder into a large bowl and add the butter, caster sugar, eggs and vanilla extract. Beat well until the mixture is smooth, then stir in the orange rind and 100g/3½ oz of the blueberries. Spoon the mixture into the paper cases.

Bake in the preheated oven for 15–20 minutes, or until risen, firm and golden brown. Transfer the cupcakes to a wire rack and leave to cool.

For the frosting, stir the soured cream into the icing sugar and mix well until smooth. Spoon a little frosting on top of each cupcake and top with the remaining blueberries. Leave to set.

variation
top the cupcakes with melted white chocolate instead

Gooey Chocolate & Cream Cheese Cupcakes

Makes 12

175 g/6 oz plain flour

20 g/¾ oz cocoa powder

¾ tsp bicarbonate of soda

200 g/7 oz caster sugar

50 ml/2 fl oz sunflower oil

175 ml/6 fl oz water

2 tsp white vinegar

½ tsp vanilla extract

150 g/5½ oz full-fat cream cheese

1 egg, lightly beaten

100 g/3½ oz plain chocolate chips

Preheat the oven to 180°C/350°F/Gas Mark 4. Put 12 paper cases in a muffin tin.

Sift the flour, cocoa powder and bicarbonate of soda into a large bowl. Stir in 150 g/ 5½ oz of the sugar. Add the oil, water, vinegar and vanilla extract, then stir well together until combined.

Place the remaining sugar, the cream cheese and egg in a large bowl and beat together until well mixed. Stir in the chocolate chips.

Spoon the cake mixture into the paper cases and top each with a spoonful of the cream cheese mixture.

Bake in the preheated oven for 25 minutes, or until firm to the touch. Leave the cupcakes to cool in the tin for 10 minutes, then transfer to a wire rack to cool completely.

great tip!
for extra indulgence, serve the cupcakes with pouring cream

Chocolate & Orange Cupcakes

Makes 16

115 g/4 oz unsalted butter,
  softened
115 g/4 oz golden caster sugar
finely grated rind and juice
  of ½ orange
2 eggs, lightly beaten
115 g/4 oz self-raising flour
25 g/1 oz plain chocolate, grated
thin strips of candied orange peel,
  to decorate

Icing

115 g/4 oz plain chocolate,
  broken into pieces
25 g/1 oz unsalted butter
1 tbsp golden syrup

Preheat the oven to 180°C/350°F/Gas Mark 4. Put 16 paper cases in bun tins.

Cream together the butter, sugar and orange rind until pale and fluffy. Gradually beat in the eggs. Sift in the flour and, using a metal spoon, fold gently into the mixture with the orange juice and grated chocolate. Spoon the mixture into the paper cases.

Bake in the preheated oven for 20 minutes, or until risen and golden brown. Transfer to a wire rack and leave to cool.

To make the icing, put the chocolate into a heatproof bowl and add the butter and golden syrup. Set the bowl over a saucepan of gently simmering water and heat until melted. Remove from the heat and stir until smooth. Leave to cool until the icing is thick enough to spread. Spread over the cupcakes and decorate each cupcake with a few strips of candied orange peel. Leave to set.

Maple Pecan Cupcakes

Makes 30

175 g/6 oz plain flour

1 tbsp baking powder

175 g/6 oz unsalted butter, softened

115 g/4 oz light muscovado sugar

4 tbsp maple syrup

3 eggs, beaten

1 tsp vanilla extract

30 g/1 oz pecan nuts, finely chopped

Topping

40 g/1½ oz pecan nuts, finely chopped

2 tbsp plain flour

2 tbsp light muscovado sugar

2 tbsp melted unsalted butter

Preheat the oven to 190°C/375°F/Gas Mark 5. Put 30 paper cases in bun tins.

Sift the flour and baking powder into a large bowl and add the butter, sugar, maple syrup, eggs and vanilla extract. Beat well until the mixture is smooth, then stir in the pecan nuts. Spoon the mixture into the paper cases.

For the topping, mix together the pecan nuts, flour, sugar and melted butter to make a crumbly mixture and spoon a little on top of each cupcake.

Bake in the preheated oven for 15–20 minutes, or until risen, firm and golden brown. Transfer to a wire rack and leave to cool.

great tip!
brush the tops of the cupcakes with maple syrup to glaze

Black Forest Cupcakes

Makes 12

85 g/3 oz plain chocolate, broken into pieces

1 tsp lemon juice

4 tbsp milk

150 g/5½ oz self-raising flour

1 tbsp cocoa powder, plus extra for dusting

½ tsp bicarbonate of soda

2 eggs

55 g/2 oz butter, softened

115 g/4 oz soft light brown sugar

25 g/1 oz dried sweetened sour cherries, chopped

2 tbsp cherry liqueur (optional)

150 ml/5 fl oz double cream, softly whipped

5 tbsp cherry conserve

Preheat the oven to 180°C/350°F/Gas Mark 4. Put 12 paper cases in a muffin tin.

Put the chocolate into a heatproof bowl and set the bowl over a saucepan of gently simmering water until melted. Remove from the heat and leave to cool slightly. Meanwhile, add the lemon juice to the milk and leave for 10 minutes – it will curdle a little.

Sift the flour, cocoa powder and bicarbonate of soda into a bowl. Add the eggs, butter, sugar and the milk mixture and beat with an electric mixer until smooth. Fold in the melted chocolate and the sour cherries. Spoon the mixture into the paper cases.

Bake in the preheated oven for 20–25 minutes, until risen and firm to the touch. Transfer to a wire rack and leave to cool.

When the cupcakes are cold, use a serrated knife to cut a circle from the top of each cupcake. Sprinkle the cakes with a little cherry liqueur, if using. Spoon the whipped cream into the centres and top with a small spoonful of conserve. Gently replace the cupcake tops and dust lightly with cocoa powder. Store in the refrigerator until ready to serve.

Carrot Cake Cupcakes

Makes 12

175 g/6 oz unsalted butter, softened

115 g/4 oz golden caster sugar

2 eggs, lightly beaten

300 g/10½ oz carrots, grated

55 g/2 oz walnuts, finely chopped

2 tbsp orange juice

grated rind of ½ orange

175 g/6 oz self-raising flour

1 tsp ground cinnamon

walnut halves, to decorate

Frosting

115 g/4 oz full-fat cream cheese

225 g/8 oz icing sugar

1 tbsp orange juice

Preheat the oven to 180°C/350°F/Gas Mark 4. Put 12 paper cases in a muffin tin.

Cream together the butter and sugar until pale and fluffy. Gradually beat in the eggs. Fold in the grated carrots, chopped walnuts, and orange juice and rind. Sift in the flour and cinnamon and, using a metal spoon, fold into the mixture until just combined. Spoon the mixture into the paper cases.

Bake in the preheated oven for 15–20 minutes, or until golden brown and firm to the touch. Transfer to a wire rack and leave to cool.

To make the frosting, place the cream cheese, icing sugar and orange juice in a bowl and beat together. Spread over the top of the cupcakes, then decorate with walnut halves.

great tip!
top the cupcakes with little carrot decorations, available from most supermarkets

Spiced Apple Pie Cupcakes

Makes 12

50 g/1¾ oz unsalted butter,
  softened
70 g/2½ oz demerara sugar
1 egg, lightly beaten
150 g/5½ oz plain flour
1½ tsp baking powder
½ tsp ground mixed spice
1 large cooking apple, peeled,
  cored and finely chopped
1 tbsp orange juice

Topping

40 g/1½ oz plain flour
½ tsp ground mixed spice
40 g/1½ oz caster sugar
25 g/1 oz unsalted butter

Preheat the oven to 180°C/350°F/Gas Mark 4. Put 12 paper cases in a muffin tin.

To make the topping, place the flour, mixed spice and caster sugar in a large bowl. Add the butter and rub in with your fingertips until the mixture resembles fine breadcrumbs. Set aside.

Cream together the butter and demerara sugar until pale and fluffy. Gradually beat in the egg. Sift in the flour, baking powder and mixed spice and fold into the mixture, then fold in the apple and orange juice. Spoon the mixture into the paper cases. Sprinkle the topping over the cupcakes and press down gently.

Bake in the preheated oven for 30 minutes, or until golden brown. Leave the cupcakes in the tin for 5 minutes, then serve warm or transfer to a wire rack and leave to cool.

Low-fat Blueberry Muffins

Makes 12

oil or melted butter, for greasing
(if using)
225 g/8 oz plain flour
1 tsp bicarbonate of soda
¼ tsp salt
1 tsp allspice
115 g/4 oz caster sugar
3 large egg whites
3 tbsp low-fat margarine
150 ml/5 fl oz thick low-fat
natural yogurt or blueberry-
flavoured yogurt
1 tsp vanilla extract
85 g/3 oz fresh blueberries

Preheat the oven to 190°C/375°F/Gas Mark 5. Put 12 paper cases in a muffin tin or brush the holes with oil or melted butter.

Sift the flour, bicarbonate of soda, salt and half the allspice into a large mixing bowl. Add 6 tablespoons of the sugar and mix together well.

In a separate bowl, whisk the egg whites together. Add the margarine, yogurt and vanilla extract and mix together well, then stir in the blueberries until thoroughly incorporated. Add the fruit mixture to the dry ingredients. Stir gently until just combined; do not over-mix.

Spoon the mixture into the prepared muffin tin. Mix the remaining sugar with the remaining allspice, then sprinkle the mixture over the muffins.

Bake in the preheated oven for 25 minutes, or until risen and golden. Leave the muffins in the tin for 5 minutes, then serve warm or transfer to a wire rack and leave to cool.

Mint Chocolate Chip Muffins

Makes 12

oil or melted butter,
    for greasing (if using)

280 g/10 oz plain flour

1 tbsp baking powder

pinch of salt

115 g/4 oz caster sugar

150 g/5½ oz plain chocolate chips

2 eggs

250 ml/9 fl oz milk

6 tbsp sunflower oil or 85 g/
    3 oz unsalted butter, melted
    and cooled

1 tsp peppermint extract

a few drops of green food
    colouring (optional)

icing sugar, for dusting

Preheat the oven to 200°C/400°F/Gas Mark 6. Put 12 paper cases in a muffin tin or brush the holes with oil or melted butter.

Sift together the flour, baking powder and salt into a large bowl. Stir in the caster sugar and chocolate chips.

Lightly beat the eggs in a large jug or bowl, then beat in the milk, oil and peppermint extract. Add the food colouring, if using, to colour the mixture a very subtle shade of green. Make a well in the centre of the dry ingredients and pour in the beaten liquid ingredients. Stir gently until just combined; do not over-mix.

Spoon the mixture into the prepared muffin tin. Bake in the preheated oven for about 20 minutes, until well risen and firm to the touch.

Leave the muffins in the tin for 5 minutes, then serve warm or transfer to a wire rack and leave to cool. Dust with icing sugar before serving.

Dark Chocolate & Ginger Muffins

Makes 12

oil or melted butter,
    for greasing (if using)
225 g/8 oz plain flour
55 g/2 oz cocoa powder
1 tbsp baking powder
1 tbsp ground ginger
pinch of salt
115 g/4 oz soft dark brown sugar
3 pieces preserved ginger in
    syrup, finely chopped,
    plus 2 tbsp syrup from the jar
2 eggs
220 ml/7½ fl oz milk
6 tbsp sunflower oil or 85 g/
    3 oz unsalted butter, melted
    and cooled

Preheat the oven to 200°C/400°F/Gas Mark 6. Put 12 paper cases in a muffin tin or brush the holes with oil or melted butter.

Sift together the flour, cocoa powder, baking powder, ground ginger and salt into a large bowl. Stir in the sugar and preserved ginger.

Lightly beat the eggs in a large jug or bowl, then beat in the milk, oil and ginger syrup. Make a well in the centre of the dry ingredients and pour in the beaten liquid ingredients. Stir gently until just combined; do not over-mix.

Spoon the mixture into the prepared muffin tin. Bake in the preheated oven for about 20 minutes, until well risen and firm to the touch.

Leave the muffins in the tin for 5 minutes, then serve warm or transfer to a wire rack and leave to cool.

Rocky Road Chocolate Muffins

Makes 12

oil or melted butter, for greasing
  (if using)
225 g/8 oz plain flour
55 g/2 oz cocoa powder
1 tbsp baking powder
pinch of salt
115 g/4 oz caster sugar
100 g/3½ oz white chocolate chips
50 g/1¾ oz white mini
  marshmallows, cut in half
2 eggs
250 ml/9 fl oz milk
6 tbsp sunflower oil or 85 g/3 oz
  unsalted butter, melted
  and cooled

Preheat the oven to 200°C/400°F/Gas Mark 6. Put 12 paper cases in a muffin tin or brush the holes with oil or melted butter.

Sift together the flour, cocoa powder, baking powder and salt into a large bowl. Stir in the sugar, chocolate chips and marshmallows.

Lightly beat the eggs in a large jug or bowl, then beat in the milk and oil. Make a well in the centre of the dry ingredients and pour in the beaten liquid ingredients. Stir gently until just combined; do not over-mix.

Spoon the mixture into the prepared muffin tin. Bake in the preheated oven for about 20 minutes, until risen and firm to the touch.

Leave the muffins in the tin for 5 minutes, then serve warm or transfer to a wire rack and leave to cool.

variation
use 55 g/2 oz chocolate
chips and add 85 g/
3 oz chopped Brazil nuts

Lemon & Poppy Seed Muffins

Makes 12

oil or melted butter,
    for greasing (if using)

280 g/10 oz plain flour

1 tbsp baking powder

pinch of salt

115 g/4 oz caster sugar

2 tbsp poppy seeds

2 eggs

250 ml/9 fl oz milk

6 tbsp sunflower oil or 85 g/
    3 oz unsalted butter, melted
    and cooled

finely grated rind of 2 lemons

Preheat the oven to 200°C/400°F/Gas Mark 6. Put 12 paper cases in a muffin tin or brush the holes with oil or melted butter.

Sift together the flour, baking powder and salt into a large bowl. Stir in the sugar and poppy seeds.

Lightly beat the eggs in a large jug or bowl, then beat in the milk, oil and lemon rind. Make a well in the centre of the dry ingredients and pour in the beaten liquid ingredients. Stir gently until just combined; do not over-mix.

Spoon the mixture into the prepared muffin tin. Bake in the preheated oven for about 20 minutes, until well risen, golden brown and firm to the touch.

Leave the muffins in the tin for 5 minutes, then serve warm or transfer to a wire rack and leave to cool.

variation
use lime rind instead of the lemon rind

Toasted Almond & Apricot Muffins

Makes 12

100 g/3½ oz dried apricots

3 tbsp orange juice

oil or melted butter,
  for greasing (if using)

50 g/1¾ oz blanched almonds

280 g/10 oz plain flour

1 tbsp baking powder

pinch of salt

115 g/4 oz caster sugar

2 eggs

200 ml/7 fl oz buttermilk

6 tbsp sunflower oil or 85 g/
  3 oz unsalted butter, melted
  and cooled

¼ tsp almond extract

40 g/1½ oz flaked almonds

Cut the apricots into small pieces and put in a bowl. Add the orange juice and leave to soak for 1 hour.

Put 12 paper cases in a muffin tin or brush the holes with oil or melted butter.

Meanwhile, toast the almonds under a preheated grill, turning frequently, until golden. When cool, chop the almonds roughly.

Preheat the oven to 200°C/400°F/Gas Mark 6. Sift together the flour, baking powder and salt into a large bowl. Stir in the sugar and chopped almonds.

Lightly beat the eggs in a large jug or bowl, then beat in the buttermilk, oil and almond extract. Make a well in the centre of the dry ingredients, pour in the beaten liquid ingredients and add the soaked apricots. Stir gently until just combined; do not over-mix.

Spoon the mixture into the prepared muffin tin. Sprinkle the flaked almonds over the tops of the muffins. Bake in the preheated oven for about 20 minutes, until well risen, golden brown and firm to the touch.

Leave the muffins in the tin for 5 minutes, then serve warm or transfer to a wire rack and leave to cool.

Crunchy Peanut Butter Muffins

Makes 12

oil or melted butter,
   for greasing (if using)

280 g/10 oz plain flour

1 tbsp baking powder

pinch of salt

115 g/4 oz soft dark brown sugar

2 eggs

175 ml/6 fl oz milk

6 tbsp sunflower oil or 85 g/
   3 oz unsalted butter, melted
   and cooled

175 g/6 oz crunchy peanut butter

Peanut topping

50 g/1¾ oz unsalted roasted
   peanuts

40 g/1½ oz demerara sugar

Preheat the oven to 200°C/400°F/Gas Mark 6. Put 12 paper cases in a muffin tin or brush the holes with oil or melted butter.

To make the peanut topping, finely chop the peanuts. Put in a bowl, add the demerara sugar and mix together. Set aside.

Sift together the flour, baking powder and salt into a large bowl. Stir in the brown sugar.

Lightly beat the eggs in a large jug or bowl, then beat in the milk, oil and peanut butter. Make a well in the centre of the dry ingredients and pour in the beaten liquid ingredients. Stir gently until just combined; do not over-mix.

Spoon the mixture into the prepared muffin tin. Sprinkle the peanut topping over the tops of the muffins. Bake in the preheated oven for about 20 minutes, until well risen, golden brown and firm to the touch.

Leave the muffins in the tin for 5 minutes, then serve warm or transfer to a wire rack and leave to cool.

Raspberry Crumble Muffins

Makes 12

oil or melted butter,
    for greasing (if using)
280 g/10 oz plain flour
1 tbsp baking powder
½ tsp bicarbonate of soda
pinch of salt
115 g/4 oz caster sugar
2 eggs
250 ml/9 fl oz natural yogurt
6 tbsp sunflower oil or 85 g/
    3 oz unsalted butter, melted
    and cooled
1 tsp vanilla extract
150 g/5½ oz frozen raspberries

Crumble topping

50 g/1¾ oz plain flour
35 g/1¼ oz unsalted butter, diced
25 g/1 oz caster sugar

Preheat the oven to 200°C/400°F/Gas Mark 6. Put 12 paper cases in a muffin tin or brush the holes with oil or melted butter.

To make the crumble topping, put the flour into a bowl. Add the butter and rub it in with your fingertips until the mixture resembles fine breadcrumbs. Stir in the sugar and set aside.

Sift together the flour, baking powder, bicarbonate of soda and salt into a large bowl. Stir in the sugar.

Lightly beat the eggs in a large jug or bowl, then beat in the yogurt, oil and vanilla extract. Make a well in the centre of the dry ingredients, pour in the beaten liquid ingredients and add the raspberries. Stir gently until just combined; do not over-mix.

Spoon the mixture into the prepared muffin tin. Sprinkle the topping over the muffins and press down lightly. Bake in the preheated oven for about 20 minutes, until well risen, golden brown and firm to the touch.

Leave the muffins in the tin for 5 minutes, then serve warm or transfer to a wire rack and leave to cool.

Cranberry & Orange Muffins

Makes 12
200 g/7 oz dried cranberries
3 tbsp orange juice
oil or melted butter,
    for greasing (if using)
280 g/10 oz plain flour
1 tbsp baking powder
pinch of salt
115 g/4 oz caster sugar
2 eggs
200 ml/7 fl oz milk
6 tbsp sunflower oil or 85 g/
    3 oz unsalted butter, melted
    and cooled
finely grated rind of 1 orange

Put the cranberries in a bowl, add the orange juice and leave to soak for 1 hour.

Put 12 paper cases in a muffin tin or brush the holes with oil or melted butter.

Preheat the oven to 200°C/400°F/Gas Mark 6. Sift together the flour, baking powder and salt into a large bowl. Stir in the sugar.

Lightly beat the eggs in a large jug or bowl, then beat in the milk, oil and orange rind. Make a well in the centre of the dry ingredients, pour in the beaten liquid ingredients and add the soaked cranberries. Stir gently until just combined; do not over-mix.

Spoon the mixture into the prepared muffin tin. Bake in the preheated oven for about 20 minutes, until well risen, golden brown and firm to the touch.

Leave the muffins in the tin for 5 minutes, then serve warm or transfer to a wire rack and leave to cool.

Chilli Cornbread Muffins

Makes 12

oil or melted butter,
    for greasing (if using)
175 g/6 oz plain flour
4 tsp baking powder
1 tsp salt
175 g/6 oz cornmeal or polenta
2 tbsp caster sugar
4 spring onions, finely chopped
1 fresh red chilli, deseeded and
    finely chopped
3 eggs
150 ml/5 fl oz natural yogurt
150 ml/5 fl oz milk

Preheat the oven to 200°C/400°F/Gas Mark 6. Put 12 paper cases in a muffin tin or brush the holes with oil or melted butter.

Sift together the flour, baking powder and salt into a large bowl. Stir in the cornmeal, sugar, spring onions and chilli.

Lightly beat the eggs in a large jug or bowl, then beat in the yogurt and milk. Make a well in the centre of the dry ingredients and pour in the beaten liquid ingredients. Stir gently until just combined; do not over-mix.

Spoon the mixture into the prepared muffin tin. Bake in the preheated oven for 15–20 minutes, until well risen, golden brown and firm to the touch.

Leave the muffins in the tin for 5 minutes, then serve warm or transfer to a wire rack and leave to cool.

great tip!
dust the tops of the muffins
with chilli powder or paprika

Brownies &
Bars

Chocolate Nut Brownies

Makes 16

225 g/8 oz plain chocolate,
   broken into pieces

175 g/6 oz unsalted butter,
   plus extra for greasing

3 large eggs

100 g/3½ oz caster sugar

175 g/6 oz self-raising flour

100 g/3½ oz walnuts or blanched
   hazelnuts, chopped

50 g/1¾ oz milk chocolate chips

Preheat the oven to 180°C/350°F/Gas Mark 4. Lightly grease a 25-cm/10-inch square shallow cake tin.

Put the chocolate in a heatproof bowl and add the butter. Set the bowl over a saucepan of gently simmering water and heat until melted. Remove from the heat and stir until smooth. Leave to cool slightly.

Meanwhile, beat together the eggs and sugar in a bowl until pale and frothy. Stir in the melted chocolate mixture and then add the flour, walnuts and chocolate chips. Mix everything together well.

Spoon the mixture into the prepared tin. Bake in the preheated oven for 30 minutes, or until the top is set and the centre is still slightly sticky. Leave to cool in the tin, then turn out and cut into squares.

great tip!
don't worry if the brownies
sink or crack as they cool —
this is normal

Marbled Chocolate Cheesecake Brownies

Makes 12

175 g/6 oz unsalted butter,
plus extra for greasing
3 tbsp cocoa powder
200 g/7 oz caster sugar
2 eggs, lightly beaten
125 g/4½ oz plain flour

Cheesecake swirl
250 g/9 oz ricotta cheese
40 g/1½ oz caster sugar
1 egg

Preheat the oven to 180°C/350°F/Gas Mark 4.
Grease a 28 x 18-cm/11 x 7-inch baking tin.

Place the butter in a saucepan and heat gently
until melted. Remove from the heat and stir in
the cocoa powder and sugar. Beat in the eggs,
add the flour and stir to mix evenly. Spoon the
mixture into the prepared tin.

For the cheesecake swirl, place the ricotta,
sugar and egg in a bowl and beat together,
then drop teaspoonfuls of the mixture over
the chocolate mixture. Use a palette knife
to swirl the mixtures together lightly.

Bake in the preheated oven for 40–45 minutes,
or until just firm to the touch. Leave to cool in
the tin, then turn out and cut into bars.

variation
fold 40 g/1½ oz chocolate
chips into the cheesecake mix

Chocolate Fudge Brownies

Makes 16

200 g/7 oz low-fat cream cheese

½ tsp vanilla extract

225 g/8 oz caster sugar

2 eggs

85 g/3 oz unsalted butter, plus
 extra for greasing

3 tbsp cocoa powder

100 g/3½ oz self-raising flour

50 g/1¾ oz pecan nuts, chopped

pecan nut halves, to decorate

Fudge icing

55 g/2 oz unsalted butter

1 tbsp milk

75 g/2¾ oz icing sugar

2 tbsp cocoa powder

Preheat the oven to 180°C/350°F/Gas Mark 4. Lightly grease and line a 20-cm/ 8-inch square shallow cake tin.

Place the cream cheese, vanilla extract and 5 teaspoons of the caster sugar in a large bowl and beat together until smooth.

Place the eggs and the remaining sugar in a separate bowl and beat together until pale and frothy. Place the butter and cocoa powder in a small saucepan and heat gently, stirring, until the butter melts and the mixture combines. Remove from the heat, then stir into the egg mixture. Fold in the flour and chopped pecan nuts.

Spoon half of the mixture into the prepared tin and smooth level. Carefully spread the cream cheese mixture over the top, then cover with the remaining mixture. Bake in the preheated oven for 40–45 minutes. Leave to cool in the tin.

To make the icing, melt the butter in a saucepan with the milk. Stir in the icing sugar and cocoa powder. Spread the icing over the brownies and decorate with pecan nut halves. Leave to set, then cut into squares.

Cappuccino Brownies

Makes 15

225 g/8 oz self-raising flour

1 tsp baking powder

1 tsp cocoa powder, plus extra
for dusting

225 g/8 oz unsalted butter,
softened, plus extra for greasing

225 g/8 oz caster sugar

4 eggs, lightly beaten

3 tbsp instant coffee granules,
dissolved in 2 tbsp hot water,
cooled

White chocolate frosting

115 g/4 oz white chocolate,
broken into pieces

55 g/2 oz unsalted butter, softened

3 tbsp milk

175 g/6 oz icing sugar

Preheat the oven to 180°C/350°F/Gas Mark 4. Grease and line the base of a 28 x 18-cm/ 11 x 7-inch shallow baking tin.

Sift the flour, baking powder and cocoa into a bowl and add the butter, caster sugar, eggs and coffee. Beat well until smooth, then spoon into the prepared tin and smooth level.

Bake in the preheated oven for 35–40 minutes, or until risen and firm to the touch. Cool in the tin for 10 minutes, then turn out and cool completely on a wire rack.

To make the frosting, place the chocolate, butter and milk in a saucepan and heat gently, stirring, until the chocolate has melted. Remove the pan from the heat and sift in the icing sugar. Beat until smooth, then spread over the top of the cake. Dust with cocoa powder and cut into squares.

Apple & Walnut Blondies

Makes 9

125 g/4½ oz unsalted butter,
   softened, plus extra for greasing
200 g/7 oz soft light brown sugar
2 large eggs, lightly beaten
1 tsp vanilla extract
250 g/9 oz plain flour
1 tsp baking powder
1 small cooking apple, peeled,
   cored and finely chopped
100 g/3½ oz walnuts,
   roughly chopped
icing sugar, for dusting

Preheat the oven to 180°C/350°F/Gas Mark 4. Grease and line a 20-cm/8-inch square shallow cake tin.

Cream together the butter and sugar until pale and fluffy. Gradually add the eggs and vanilla extract, beating well after each addition.

Sift in the flour and baking powder and fold in evenly. Add the apple and walnuts to the mixture and stir together until well mixed.

Spoon the mixture into the prepared tin and smooth level. Bake in the preheated oven for 40–45 minutes, or until risen and golden brown. Leave to cool in the tin, then dust with icing sugar and cut into squares.

great tip!
don't chop the walnuts
too finely

Chocolate Chip & Ginger Blondies

Makes 9

125 g/4½ oz unsalted butter, softened, plus extra for greasing

200 g/7 oz soft light brown sugar

2 large eggs, lightly beaten

250 g/9 oz plain flour

1 tsp baking powder

1 tsp ground ginger

4 pieces stem ginger in syrup, drained and finely chopped

100 g/3½ oz plain chocolate chips

icing sugar, for dusting

Preheat the oven to 180°C/350°F/Gas Mark 4. Grease and line a 20-cm/8-inch square shallow cake tin.

Cream together the butter and brown sugar until pale and fluffy. Gradually add the eggs, beating well after each addition. Sift in the flour, baking powder and ground ginger and beat together until mixed. Add the stem ginger and chocolate chips and stir together until well mixed. Spoon the mixture into the prepared tin and smooth level.

Bake in the preheated oven for 40–45 minutes or until risen and golden brown. Leave to cool in the tin, then dust with icing sugar and cut into squares.

variation
use white chocolate chips instead of plain chocolate ones

Banana & Carrot Squares

Makes 16

175 g/6 oz plain flour

1 tbsp baking powder

1 tsp ground nutmeg

175 g/6 oz unsalted butter,
softened, plus extra for greasing

175 g/6 oz golden caster sugar

3 eggs, beaten

1 tbsp lemon juice

1 banana, mashed

140 g/5 oz carrots, coarsely grated

40 g/1½ oz walnuts, finely chopped

dried banana chips and freshly
grated nutmeg, to decorate

Frosting

250 g/9 oz ricotta cheese

70 g/2½ oz icing sugar

finely grated rind of ½ lemon

Preheat the oven to 160°C/325°F/Gas Mark 3. Grease and line a 23-cm/9-inch square cake tin.

Sift the flour, baking powder and nutmeg into a bowl and add the butter, caster sugar and eggs. Beat well until smooth, then stir in the lemon juice, mashed banana, grated carrots and walnuts.

Spoon the mixture into the prepared tin and smooth level. Bake in the preheated oven for 45–55 minutes, or until risen, firm and golden brown.

Cool in the tin for 5 minutes, then turn out and cool completely on a wire rack. Cut into squares when cold.

For the frosting, mix the ricotta with the icing sugar and lemon rind in a small bowl. Pipe or spoon a little frosting on top of each square of cake, top with a banana chip and sprinkle with nutmeg.

Lemon Drizzle Bars

Makes 12

2 eggs

175 g/6 oz caster sugar

150 g/5½ oz soft margarine,
    plus extra for greasing

finely grated rind of 1 lemon

175 g/6 oz self-raising flour

125 ml/4 fl oz milk

icing sugar, for dusting

Syrup

140 g/5 oz icing sugar

50 ml/2 fl oz lemon juice

Preheat the oven to 180°C/350°F/Gas Mark 4. Grease and line an 18-cm/7-inch square cake tin.

Place the eggs, caster sugar and margarine in a large bowl and beat well until smooth and fluffy. Stir in the lemon rind, then fold in the flour lightly and evenly. Stir in the milk, mixing evenly, then spoon the mixture into the prepared cake tin and smooth level.

Bake in the preheated oven for 45–50 minutes, or until golden brown and firm to the touch. Remove from the oven and stand the tin on a wire rack.

To make the syrup, place the icing sugar and lemon juice in a small saucepan and heat gently, stirring until the sugar dissolves. Do not boil.

Prick the warm cake all over with a skewer, and spoon the hot syrup evenly over the top, allowing it to be absorbed.

Leave to cool completely in the tin, then turn out the cake, cut into bars and dust with icing sugar.

Coconut Bars

Makes 10

125 g/4½ oz unsalted butter,
   plus extra for greasing
225 g/8 oz golden caster sugar
2 eggs, lightly beaten
finely grated rind of 1 orange
3 tbsp orange juice
150 ml/5 fl oz soured cream
140 g/5 oz self-raising flour
85 g/3 oz desiccated coconut
toasted shredded coconut,
   to decorate

Frosting

1 egg white
200 g/7 oz icing sugar
85 g/3 oz desiccated coconut
about 1 tbsp orange juice

Preheat the oven to 180°C/350°F/Gas Mark 4. Grease and line the base of a 23-cm/9-inch square cake tin.

Cream together the butter and caster sugar until pale and fluffy. Gradually add the eggs, beating well after each addition. Stir in the orange rind, orange juice and soured cream. Fold in the flour and desiccated coconut evenly, then spoon the mixture into the prepared tin and smooth level.

Bake in the preheated oven for 35–40 minutes, or until risen and firm to the touch. Cool in the tin for 10 minutes, then turn out and cool completely on a wire rack.

To make the frosting, place the egg white in a bowl and beat lightly, just enough to break it up. Stir in the icing sugar and desiccated coconut and add enough orange juice to mix to a thick paste. Spread over the top of the cake, sprinkle with toasted shredded coconut, then leave to set before slicing into bars.

Carrot Bars

Makes 14–16

175 g/6 oz unsalted butter, plus
    extra for greasing

85 g/3 oz light muscovado sugar

2 eggs, beaten

55 g/2 oz self-raising
    wholemeal flour

1 tsp baking powder

1 tsp ground cinnamon

115 g/4 oz ground almonds

115 g/4 oz carrot, coarsely
    grated

85 g/3 oz sultanas

85 g/3 oz ready-to-eat dried
    apricots, finely chopped

55 g/2 oz toasted chopped
    hazelnuts

1 tbsp flaked almonds

Preheat the oven to 180°C/350°F/Gas Mark 4. Grease and line a 25 x 20-cm/ 10 x 8-inch shallow baking tin.

Cream together the butter and sugar until pale and fluffy. Gradually add the eggs, beating well after each addition.

Sift in the flour, baking powder and cinnamon and fold in lightly and evenly with a metal spoon. Fold in the ground almonds, grated carrot, sultanas, apricots and hazelnuts.

Spoon the mixture into the prepared tin and sprinkle the flaked almonds over the top. Bake in the preheated oven for 35–45 minutes, or until a skewer inserted into the centre comes out clean.

Remove from the oven and leave to cool in the tin, then turn out and cut into bars.

Coconut Paradise Slices

Makes 16

200 g/7 oz plain chocolate,
   broken into pieces
100 g/3½ oz unsalted butter,
   plus extra for greasing
200 g/7 oz caster sugar
2 large eggs, lightly beaten
200 g/7 oz desiccated coconut
100 g/3½ oz sultanas
100 g/3½ oz glacé cherries

Grease and line a 23-cm/9-inch square cake tin. Place the chocolate in a heatproof bowl, set the bowl over a saucepan of gently simmering water and heat until melted. Remove from the heat and stir until smooth. Pour into the prepared tin and leave to set for about 1 hour.

Preheat the oven to 180°C/350°F/Gas Mark 4. Cream together the butter and sugar until pale and fluffy. Gradually add the eggs, beating well after each addition. Add the desiccated coconut, sultanas and glacé cherries and stir together until combined. Spoon the mixture into the tin on top of the chocolate and spread out evenly.

Bake in the preheated oven for 30–35 minutes, or until golden brown. Leave to cool in the tin, then turn out and cut into slices.

great tip!
when melting chocolate, make
sure the base of the bowl does
not touch the water

Sticky Pecan Pie Slices

Makes 10

115 g/4 oz cold unsalted butter, diced, plus extra for greasing

175 g/6 oz plain flour

130 g/4¾ oz soft light brown sugar

2 large eggs

50 g/1¾ oz pecan nuts, chopped

175 g/6 oz golden syrup

½ tsp vanilla extract

Preheat the oven to 190°C/375°F/Gas Mark 5. Grease and line a shallow 23-cm/9-inch square cake tin. Grease the paper. Place 25 g/1 oz of the butter in a saucepan and heat gently until melted. Leave to cool slightly.

Sift the flour into a large bowl, add the remaining butter and rub it in with your fingertips until the mixture resembles fine breadcrumbs. Stir in 40 g/1½ oz of the sugar, then spoon the mixture into the tin and press down firmly with the back of a spoon. Bake in the preheated oven for 20 minutes.

Meanwhile, place the eggs in a large bowl and beat lightly. Add the remaining sugar, the pecan nuts, melted butter, golden syrup and vanilla extract and stir together until combined.

Pour the mixture over the base and bake in the oven for a further 15–20 minutes, or until firm to the touch and golden brown. Remove from the tin and leave to cool. When cold, cut into slices to serve.

Bakewell Slices

Makes 12

175 g/6 oz plain flour, plus extra
   for dusting
125 g/4½ oz cold unsalted butter
25 g/1 oz caster sugar
1 egg yolk
about 1 tbsp cold water

Filling

115 g/4 oz unsalted butter
115 g/4 oz caster sugar
115 g/4 oz ground almonds
3 eggs, beaten
½ tsp almond extract
4 tbsp raspberry jam
2 tbsp flaked almonds

Sift the flour into a bowl and rub in the butter with your fingertips until the mixture resembles fine breadcrumbs. Stir in the sugar, then mix the egg yolk with the water and stir in to make a firm dough. Wrap in clingfilm and chill for about 15 minutes.

Preheat the oven to 200°C/400°F/Gas Mark 6. Roll out the dough on a lightly floured surface and use to line a 23-cm/9-inch square tart tin. Prick the base of the pastry case all over and chill for 15 minutes.

Meanwhile, cream together the butter and sugar until pale and fluffy, then beat in the ground almonds, eggs and almond extract.

Spread the jam over the base of the pastry case, then top with the almond mixture, spreading evenly. Sprinkle the flaked almonds over the top.

Bake in the preheated oven for 10 minutes, then reduce the heat to 180°C/350°F/Gas Mark 4 and bake for a further 25–30 minutes, or until the filling is golden brown and firm to the touch. Leave to cool in the tin, then cut into bars.

Strawberry Chocolate Slices

Makes 16

225 g/8 oz plain flour

1 tsp baking powder

100 g/3½ oz caster sugar

85 g/3 oz soft light brown sugar

225 g/8 oz unsalted butter

150 g/5½ oz rolled oats

225 g/8 oz strawberry jam

100 g/3½ oz plain chocolate chips

25 g/1 oz flaked almonds

Preheat the oven to 190°C/375°F/Gas Mark 5. Line a 30 x 20-cm/12 x 8-inch baking tin.

Sift the flour and baking powder into a large bowl, add the sugars and mix well. Add the butter and rub it in with your fingertips until the mixture resembles breadcrumbs. Stir in the oats, then press three quarters of the mixture into the base of the prepared tin. Bake in the preheated oven for 10 minutes.

Spread the jam over the cooked base and sprinkle over the chocolate chips. Place the remaining flour mixture and the flaked almonds in a bowl and mix together, then sprinkle evenly over the chocolate chips and press down lightly. Bake for a further 20–25 minutes, or until golden brown. Leave to cool in the tin, then cut into slices.

variation
replace the strawberry jam with apricot jam

Chocolate Peppermint Bars

Makes 16

55 g/2 oz unsalted butter,
plus extra for greasing
55 g/2 oz caster sugar
115 g/4 oz plain flour
175 g/6 oz icing sugar
1–2 tbsp warm water
½ tsp peppermint extract
2 tsp green food colouring
(optional)
175 g/6 oz plain chocolate,
broken into pieces

Preheat the oven to 180°C/350°F/Gas Mark 4. Grease and line a 30 x 20-cm/ 12 x 8-inch shallow baking tin.

Cream together the butter and sugar until pale and fluffy. Stir in the flour until the mixture binds together.

Knead the mixture to form a smooth dough, then press over the base of the prepared tin and prick all over with a fork. Bake in the preheated oven for 10–15 minutes, or until lightly browned and just firm to the touch. Leave to cool in the tin.

Sift the icing sugar into a bowl. Gradually add the water, then add the peppermint extract and food colouring, if using. Spread the icing over the base, then leave to set.

Place the chocolate in a heatproof bowl, set the bowl over a saucepan of gently simmering water and heat until melted. Spread the melted chocolate over the icing. Leave to set, then cut into slices.

Caramel Chocolate Shortbread

Makes 12

115 g/4 oz unsalted butter,
plus extra for greasing
175 g/6 oz plain flour
55 g/2 oz golden caster sugar

Filling & topping

200 g/7 oz butter
115 g/4 oz golden caster sugar
3 tbsp golden syrup
400 g/14 oz canned
condensed milk
200 g/7 oz plain chocolate,
broken into pieces

Preheat the oven to 180°C/350°F/Gas
Mark 4. Grease and line the base of a
23-cm/9-inch square shallow cake tin.

Place the butter, flour and sugar in a food
processor and process until they begin
to bind together. Press the mixture over
the base of the prepared tin. Bake in the
preheated oven for 20–25 minutes,
or until golden.

Meanwhile, make the filling. Place the butter,
sugar, golden syrup and condensed milk in
a saucepan and heat gently until the sugar
has dissolved. Bring to the boil and simmer
for 6–8 minutes, stirring constantly, until the
mixture becomes very thick. Pour the filling
over the base and chill in the refrigerator
until firm.

Place the chocolate in a heatproof bowl,
set the bowl over a saucepan of gently
simmering water and heat until melted.
Spread the melted chocolate over the filling.
Leave to set, then cut into slices.

Chocolate Peanut Butter Squares

Makes 20

300 g/10½ oz milk chocolate

350 g/12 oz plain flour

1 tsp baking powder

225 g/8 oz unsalted butter,
  plus extra for greasing

350 g/12 oz soft light
  brown sugar

175 g/6 oz rolled oats

70 g/2½ oz chopped mixed nuts

1 egg, lightly beaten

400 g/14 oz canned condensed
  milk

70 g/2½ oz crunchy
  peanut butter

Preheat the oven to 180°C/350°F/Gas Mark 4. Grease a 30 x 20-cm/12 x 8-inch shallow baking tin.

Finely chop the chocolate. Sift the flour and baking powder into a large bowl, add the butter and rub it in with your fingertips until the mixture resembles breadcrumbs. Stir in the sugar, oats and nuts. Place a quarter of the mixture into a bowl and stir in the chopped chocolate. Set aside.

Stir the egg into the remaining mixture, then press over the base of the prepared tin. Bake in the preheated oven for 15 minutes.

Meanwhile, place the condensed milk and peanut butter in a bowl and mix together. Pour the mixture over the base and spread evenly, then sprinkle the reserved chocolate mixture on top and press down lightly. Bake for a further 20 minutes, or until golden brown. Leave to cool in the tin, then cut into squares.

Nutty Flapjacks

Makes 16
200 g/7 oz rolled oats
115 g/4 oz chopped hazelnuts
55 g/2 oz plain flour
115 g/4 oz unsalted butter, plus
    extra for greasing
2 tbsp golden syrup
85 g/3 oz light muscovado sugar

Preheat the oven to 180°C/350°F/Gas Mark 4. Grease a 23-cm/9-inch square cake tin.

Place the oats, hazelnuts and flour in a large bowl and stir together.

Place the butter, golden syrup and sugar in a saucepan over a low heat and stir until melted. Pour onto the dry ingredients and mix well. Spoon the mixture into the prepared tin and smooth level.

Bake in the preheated oven for 20–25 minutes, or until golden and firm to the touch. Cut into squares and leave to cool in the tin.

variation
for fruit and nut flapjacks, add a handful of chopped dried fruit, such as dried apricots

Cookies

Chocolate Chip Cookies

Makes 18

125 g/4½ oz soft margarine,
plus extra for greasing
175 g/6 oz plain flour
1 tsp baking powder
85 g/3 oz light muscovado sugar
5 tbsp caster sugar
½ tsp vanilla extract
1 egg
125 g/4½ oz plain chocolate chips

Preheat the oven to 190°C/375°F/Gas Mark 5. Lightly grease two baking sheets.

Place all of the ingredients in a large mixing bowl and beat until well combined.

Place tablespoonfuls of the mixture onto the prepared baking sheets, spaced well apart.

Bake in the preheated oven for 10–12 minutes, or until golden brown.

Leave to cool for 5–10 minutes, then transfer to wire racks to cool completely.

variation
replace the chocolate chips
with chocolate chunks or
chopped chocolate

Crunchy Peanut Cookies

Makes 20

125 g/4½ oz unsalted butter, softened, plus extra for greasing

150 g/5½ oz chunky peanut butter

225 g/8 oz granulated sugar

1 egg, lightly beaten

150 g/5½ oz plain flour

½ tsp baking powder

pinch of salt

75 g/2¾ oz unsalted natural peanuts, chopped

Place the butter and peanut butter in a large bowl and beat together. Gradually add the sugar and beat well. Add the egg, a little at a time, until it is combined. Sift in the flour, baking powder and salt. Add the peanuts and bring all of the ingredients together to form a soft dough. Wrap the dough in clingfilm and chill in the refrigerator for 30 minutes.

Preheat the oven to 190°C/375°F/ Gas Mark 5. Lightly grease two large baking sheets.

Form the dough into balls and place them on the prepared baking sheets, spaced well apart. Flatten them slightly with your hand.

Bake in the preheated oven for 15 minutes, or until golden brown. Leave to cool for 5–10 minutes, then transfer to wire racks to cool completely.

variation
sandwich together pairs of these cookies with peanut butter and strawberry jam

Classic Oat Cookies

Makes 30

175 g/6 oz unsalted butter or
    margarine, plus extra for
    greasing
275 g/9¾ oz demerara sugar
1 egg
4 tbsp water
1 tsp vanilla extract
375 g/13 oz rolled oats
140 g/5 oz plain flour
1 tsp salt
½ tsp bicarbonate of soda

Preheat the oven to 180°C/350°F/Gas
Mark 4. Lightly grease two large
baking sheets.

Cream together the butter and sugar until
pale and fluffy. Beat in the egg, water and
vanilla extract until the mixture is smooth.

In a separate bowl, mix the oats, flour, salt
and bicarbonate of soda. Gradually stir the
oat mixture into the butter mixture until
thoroughly combined.

Put rounded tablespoonfuls of the mixture
onto the prepared baking sheet, spaced
well apart. Bake in the preheated oven for
15 minutes, or until golden brown.

Leave to cool for 5–10 minutes, then
transfer to wire racks to cool completely.

variation
add 85 g/3 oz chopped
sultanas and raisins to the
dough mix

Almond & Raspberry Jam Drops

Makes about 25

225 g/8 oz unsalted butter, softened

140 g/5 oz caster sugar

1 egg yolk, lightly beaten

2 tsp almond extract

280 g/10 oz plain flour

pinch of salt

55 g/2 oz almonds, toasted and chopped

55 g/2 oz chopped mixed peel

4 tbsp raspberry jam

Preheat the oven to 190°C/375°F/Gas Mark 5. Line two baking sheets with baking paper.

Put the butter and sugar into a bowl and mix well with a wooden spoon, then beat in the egg yolk and almond extract. Sift the flour and salt into the mixture, add the almonds and mixed peel and stir until thoroughly combined.

Scoop out tablespoons of the mixture and shape into balls with your hands, then put them on to the prepared baking sheets, spaced well apart. Use the dampened handle of a wooden spoon to make a hollow in the centre of each cookie and fill with jam.

Bake in the preheated oven for 12–15 minutes, until golden brown. Leave to cool for 5–10 minutes, then transfer to wire racks to cool completely.

variation
use your favourite jam in this recipe in place of the raspberry jam

Date & Lemon Spirals

Makes about 30

225 g/8 oz unsalted butter, softened

175 g/6 oz caster sugar

1 egg yolk, lightly beaten

1 tsp lemon extract

280 g/10 oz plain flour

pinch of salt

280 g/10 oz dried dates, stoned and finely chopped

2 tbsp clear honey

5 tbsp lemon juice

1 tbsp finely grated lemon rind

125 ml/4 fl oz water

1 tsp ground cinnamon

Put the butter and 140 g/5 oz of the sugar into a bowl and mix well, then beat in the egg yolk and lemon extract. Sift in the flour and salt, and stir until thoroughly combined. Shape the dough into a ball, wrap in clingfilm and chill for 30–60 minutes.

Meanwhile, put the dates, honey, lemon juice, lemon rind and water in a saucepan. Bring to the boil, stirring constantly, then reduce the heat and simmer gently for 5 minutes. Remove from the heat and leave to cool, then chill for 15 minutes.

Mix together the cinnamon and remaining sugar. Roll out the dough between two sheets of baking paper into a 30-cm/ 12-inch square. Sprinkle the cinnamon and sugar mixture over the dough and roll lightly with the rolling pin. Spread the date mixture evenly over the dough, then roll up like a Swiss roll. Wrap in clingfilm and chill in the refrigerator for 30 minutes.

Preheat the oven to 190°C/375°F/Gas Mark 5. Line two baking sheets with baking paper. Unwrap the roll and cut into thin slices. Place on the prepared baking sheets, spaced well apart. Bake in the preheated oven for 12–15 minutes, until golden brown. Leave to cool for 5–10 minutes, then transfer to wire racks to cool completely.

Blueberry, Cranberry & White Chocolate Cookies

Makes about 30

225 g/8 oz unsalted butter, softened

140 g/5 oz golden caster sugar

1 egg yolk, lightly beaten

2 tsp orange juice

280 g/10 oz plain flour

pinch of salt

55 g/2 oz fresh or dried blueberries

55 g/2 oz fresh or dried cranberries

25 g/1 oz white chocolate chips

Preheat the oven to 190°C/375°F/Gas Mark 5. Line two baking sheets with baking paper.

Put the butter and sugar into a bowl and mix well with a wooden spoon, then beat in the egg yolk and orange juice. Sift in the flour and salt, add the blueberries, cranberries and chocolate chips and stir until thoroughly combined. Scoop up tablespoons of the dough and put them on the prepared baking sheets, spaced well apart.

Bake in the preheated oven for 10–15 minutes, until light golden brown. Leave to cool for 5–10 minutes, then transfer to wire racks to cool completely.

variation
use 100 g/3½ oz dried sour cherries in place of the fruit, and plain chocolate chips

Melting Moments

Makes 32

350 g/12 oz unsalted butter, softened

85 g/3 oz icing sugar

½ tsp vanilla extract

300 g/10½ oz plain flour

50 g/1¾ oz cornflour

Preheat the oven to 180°C/350°F/Gas Mark 4. Line two large baking sheets with baking paper

Place the butter and icing sugar in a large bowl and beat together until light and fluffy, then beat in the vanilla extract. Sift in the flour and cornflour and mix thoroughly.

Spoon the mixture into a piping bag fitted with a large star nozzle and pipe cookies onto the prepared baking sheets, spaced well apart.

Bake in the preheated oven for 15–20 minutes or until golden brown. Leave to cool on the baking sheets.

variation
dip the cookies into melted chocolate to half-cover

Fruit & Nut Cookies

Makes 10

100 g/3½ oz plain flour

60 g/2¼ oz rolled oats

50 g/1¾ oz hazelnuts, chopped

75 g/2¾ oz ready-to-eat dried
  apricots, chopped

125 g/4½ oz unsalted butter,
  plus extra for greasing

75 g/2¾ oz soft light brown sugar

2 tbsp golden syrup

Preheat the oven to 180°C/350°F/Gas Mark 4. Lightly grease two baking sheets.

Put the flour, oats, hazelnuts and apricots in a large bowl and stir until thoroughly combined.

Put the butter, sugar and golden syrup in a saucepan and heat gently, stirring occasionally, until melted.

Pour the butter mixture into the bowl and stir to make a soft, chunky dough. Put heaped dessertspoonfuls of the mixture onto the prepared baking sheets, spaced well apart, and flatten slightly.

Bake in the preheated oven for 15 minutes, until light golden. Leave to cool for 5–10 minutes, then transfer to wire racks to cool completely.

Sparkly Stars

Makes 20

215 g/7½ oz plain flour,
    plus extra for dusting
1 tsp baking powder
pinch of salt
140 g/5 oz unsalted butter,
    diced
115 g/4 oz soft light brown sugar
1 tsp ground cinnamon
1 egg yolk
edible silver balls, to decorate

Icing

200 g/7 oz icing sugar
1 tbsp lemon juice
½ –1 tbsp water

Preheat the oven to 180°C/350°F/Gas Mark 4. Line two large baking sheets with baking paper.

Sift the flour, baking powder and salt into a large bowl. Add the butter and rub it in with your fingertips until the mixture resembles fine breadcrumbs. Stir in the brown sugar, cinnamon and egg yolk, then mix to a dough.

Roll out the dough on a lightly floured surface to about 5 mm/¼ inch thick. Stamp out cookies with a star-shaped cutter and put them on the prepared baking sheets.

Bake in the preheated oven for 15–20 minutes, until golden brown. Leave to cool for 5–10 minutes, then transfer to wire racks to cool completely.

To make the icing, put the icing sugar in a small bowl. Add the lemon juice, then gradually stir in the water to make a smooth icing. Spread a little of the icing over each cookie, then decorate with silver balls.

Cherry & Chocolate Diamonds

Makes 30

225 g/8 oz unsalted butter, softened

140 g/5 oz caster sugar

1 egg yolk, lightly beaten

2 tsp vanilla extract

280 g/10 oz plain flour

pinch of salt

55 g/2 oz glacé cherries, finely chopped

55 g/2 oz milk chocolate chips

Put the butter and sugar into a bowl and mix well with a wooden spoon, then beat in the egg yolk and vanilla extract. Sift in the flour and salt, add the glacé cherries and chocolate chips and stir until thoroughly combined. Shape the dough into a ball, wrap in clingfilm and chill for 30–60 minutes.

Preheat the oven to 190°C/375°F/Gas Mark 5. Line two baking sheets with baking paper.

Roll out the dough between two sheets of baking paper to about 3 mm/⅛ inch thick. Stamp out cookies with a diamond-shaped cutter and put them on the prepared baking sheets.

Bake in the preheated oven for 10–15 minutes, until light golden brown. Leave to cool for 5–10 minutes, then transfer to wire racks to cool completely.

Vanilla Macaroons

Makes 16

75 g/2¾ oz ground almonds
115 g/4 oz icing sugar
2 large egg whites
50 g/1¾ oz caster sugar
½ tsp vanilla extract

Filling

55 g/2 oz unsalted butter,
   softened
½ tsp vanilla extract
115 g/4 oz icing sugar

Place the ground almonds and icing sugar in a food processor and process for 15 seconds. Sift the mixture into a bowl. Line two baking sheets with baking paper.

Place the egg whites in a large bowl and whisk until holding soft peaks. Gradually whisk in the caster sugar to make a firm, glossy meringue. Whisk in the vanilla extract.

Fold the almond mixture into the meringue one third at a time. Continue to cut and fold the mixture until it forms a shiny batter with a thick, ribbon-like consistency. Spoon the mixture into a piping bag fitted with a 1-cm/½-inch plain nozzle. Pipe 32 small rounds onto the prepared baking sheets. Tap the baking sheets firmly and leave to stand for 30 minutes. Preheat the oven to 160°C/325°F/Gas Mark 3.

Bake in the preheated oven for 10–15 minutes. Leave to cool for 5–10 minutes, then transfer to wire racks to cool completely.

To make the filling, beat the butter and vanilla extract in a bowl until pale and fluffy. Gradually beat in the icing sugar until smooth. Use to sandwich pairs of macaroons together.

Halloween Spider's Web Cookies

Makes 30

225 g/8 oz unsalted butter, softened

140 g/5 oz caster sugar

1 egg yolk, lightly beaten

1 tsp peppermint extract

250 g/9 oz plain flour

25 g/1 oz cocoa powder

pinch of salt

Icing

175 g/6 oz icing sugar

a few drops of vanilla extract

1–1½ tbsp hot water

a few drops of black food colouring

Put the butter and caster sugar into a bowl and mix well, then beat in the egg yolk and peppermint extract. Sift in the flour, cocoa powder and salt, and stir until combined. Shape the dough into a ball, wrap in clingfilm and chill for 30–60 minutes.

Preheat the oven to 190°C/375°F/Gas Mark 5. Line two baking sheets with baking paper.

Roll out the dough between two sheets of baking paper. Stamp out cookies with a 6-cm/2½-inch plain round cutter and put them on the prepared baking sheets.

Bake in the preheated oven for 10–15 minutes, until light golden brown. Leave to cool for 5–10 minutes, then transfer to wire racks to cool completely.

To make the icing, sift the icing sugar into a bowl, add the vanilla extract and stir in the hot water. Spread most the icing over the cookies. Add the food colouring to the remaining icing and spoon it into a piping bag fitted with a fine nozzle. Pipe a series of concentric circles over each cookie, then carefully draw a cocktail stick through the icing from the middle to the outside edge to divide the cookie into eighths. Leave to set.

Vanilla
Hearts

Makes 12

225 g/8 oz plain flour, plus extra
  for dusting
150 g/5½ oz unsalted butter, diced,
  plus extra for greasing
125 g/4½ oz caster sugar,
  plus extra for dusting
1 tsp vanilla extract

Preheat the oven to 180°C/350°F/Gas
Mark 4. Lightly grease a baking sheet.

Sift the flour into a large bowl. Add the
butter and rub it in with your fingertips until
the mixture resembles fine breadcrumbs.
Stir in the sugar and vanilla extract and mix
together to form a firm dough.

Roll out the dough on a lightly floured
surface to about 1 cm/½ inch thick. Stamp
out cookies with a heart-shaped cutter
measuring about 5 cm/2 inches across. Put
the cookies on the prepared baking sheet.

Bake in the preheated oven for 15–20 minutes,
or until just coloured. Leave to cool for
5–10 minutes, then transfer to wire racks to
cool completely. Dust with a little sugar just
before serving.

great tip!
*place a vanilla pod in your
jar of sugar to give the sugar
a delicious vanilla flavour*

Chocolate-dipped Viennese Fingers

Makes about 16

100 g/3½ oz unsalted butter,
    plus extra for greasing
25 g/1 oz golden caster sugar
½ tsp vanilla extract
100 g/3½ oz self-raising flour
100 g/3½ oz plain chocolate,
    broken into pieces

Preheat the oven to 160°C/325°F/Gas Mark 3. Grease two large baking sheets.

Cream together the butter, sugar and vanilla extract until pale and fluffy. Stir in the flour, mixing evenly to make a fairly stiff dough.

Spoon the mixture into a piping bag fitted with a large star nozzle and pipe about 16 fingers, each 6 cm/2½ inches long, onto the prepared baking sheets.

Bake in the preheated oven for 10–15 minutes, or until pale golden. Leave to cool for 2–3 minutes, then transfer to a wire rack to cool completely.

Place the chocolate in a small heatproof bowl, set over a saucepan of gently simmering water and heat until melted. Remove from the heat. Dip the ends of each biscuit into the chocolate to coat, then place on a sheet of baking paper and leave to set.

Alphabet Cookies

Makes 30

225 g/8 oz unsalted butter, softened

140 g/5 oz caster sugar

1 egg yolk, lightly beaten

2 tsp grenadine

280 g/10 oz plain flour

a pinch of salt

5–6 tbsp unsalted dried pomegranate seeds or roasted melon seeds

Put the butter and sugar into a bowl and mix well with a wooden spoon, then beat in the egg yolk and grenadine. Sift in the flour and salt, and stir until thoroughly combined. Shape the dough into a ball, wrap in clingfilm and chill for 30–60 minutes.

Preheat the oven to 190°C/375°F/Gas Mark 5. Line two baking sheets with baking paper.

Roll out the dough between two sheets of baking paper to about 3 mm/⅛ inch thick. Sprinkle the seeds over the dough and roll lightly with the rolling pin. Stamp out letters with alphabet cutters and put them on the prepared baking sheets.

Bake in the preheated oven for 10–12 minutes, until golden brown. Leave to cool for 5–10 minutes, then transfer to wire racks to cool completely.

Stained Glass Window Cookies

Makes about 25

350 g/12 oz plain flour, plus extra
for dusting

pinch of salt

1 tsp bicarbonate of soda

100 g/3½ oz unsalted butter, diced

175 g/6 oz caster sugar

1 large egg

1 tsp vanilla extract

4 tbsp golden syrup

50 coloured boiled fruit sweets
(about 250 g/9 oz), chopped

25 lengths of ribbon, to decorate

Sift the flour, salt and bicarbonate of soda into a large bowl. Add the butter and rub it in until the mixture resembles breadcrumbs. Stir in the sugar. Place the egg, vanilla extract and golden syrup in a separate bowl and whisk together. Pour the egg mixture into the flour mixture and mix to form a smooth dough. Shape the dough into a ball, wrap in clingfilm and chill for 30 minutes.

Preheat the oven to 180°C/350°F/Gas Mark 4. Line two large baking sheets with baking paper. Roll the dough out on a lightly floured surface to about 5 mm/¼ inch thick. Stamp out cookies with a variety of different-shaped cutters.

Transfer the cookies to the prepared baking sheets and cut out shapes from the centres. Fill the holes with the chopped sweets. Using a skewer, make a hole at the top of each cookie.

Bake in the preheated oven for 10–12 minutes, or until the sweets are melted. Make sure the holes are still there, and re-pierce if necessary. Leave to cool on the baking sheets until the centres have hardened. When cold, thread lengths of ribbon through the holes to hang up the cookies.

Gingerbread People

Makes about 20
450 g/1 lb plain flour,
   plus extra for dusting
2 tsp ground ginger
1 tsp ground mixed spice
2 tsp bicarbonate of soda
115 g/4 oz unsalted butter, plus
   extra for greasing
100 g/3½ oz golden syrup
115 g/4 oz light muscovado
   sugar
1 egg, lightly beaten
currants and glacé cherries,
   to decorate

Icing
85 g/3 oz icing sugar
3–4 tsp water

Preheat the oven to 160°C/325°F/Gas Mark 3. Grease three large baking sheets.

Sift the flour, ginger, mixed spice and bicarbonate of soda into a large bowl. Place the butter, golden syrup and muscovado sugar in a saucepan over a low heat and stir until melted. Pour onto the dry ingredients and add the egg. Mix together to form a dough. The dough will be sticky to start with, but will become firmer as it cools.

Roll out the dough on a lightly floured surface to about 3 mm/⅛ inch thick. Stamp out cookies with a gingerbread man cutter and put them on the prepared baking sheets. Decorate with currants for eyes and pieces of glacé cherry for mouths.

Bake in the preheated oven for 15–20 minutes, or until firm and lightly browned. Leave to cool for 5–10 minutes, then transfer to wire racks to cool completely.

To make the icing, place the icing sugar and water in a small bowl and mix together. Spoon the icing into a small piping bag fitted with a fine nozzle and use to pipe buttons and bows onto the cookies.

Whoopie Pies

Makes 8–10

225 g/8 oz plain flour

3 tbsp cocoa powder

½ tsp bicarbonate of soda

¼ tsp salt

115 g/4 oz unsalted butter,
   softened

225 g/8 oz soft light brown sugar

1 egg

1¼ tsp vanilla extract

125 ml/4 fl oz buttermilk

Filling

115 g/4 oz cream cheese

200 g/7 oz bottled marshmallow
   crème

Preheat the oven to 190°C/375°F/Gas Mark 5. Line two baking sheets with baking paper.

Sift the flour, cocoa powder, bicarbonate of soda and salt into a mixing bowl.

In a separate bowl, cream together the butter and sugar until pale and fluffy. Beat in the egg and vanilla extract until thoroughly combined. Stir in one third of the flour mixture until combined. Add half the buttermilk and stir to mix. Stir in half the remaining flour until combined, then stir in the remaining buttermilk. Finally, mix in the remaining flour.

Spoon the mixture onto the prepared baking sheets to make rounds 1 cm/½ inch high and 7.5 cm/3 inches in diameter. Bake in the preheated oven for 12–14 minutes, until the slightly firm to the touch. Leave to cool for 15 minutes, then transfer to wire racks to cool completely.

To make the filling, beat the cream cheese in a bowl until light and fluffy. Fold in the marshmallow crème. Use to sandwich pairs of the whoopie pies together.

Snickerdoodles

Makes 40

225 g/8 oz unsalted butter,
    softened

140 g/5 oz caster sugar

2 large eggs, lightly beaten

1 tsp vanilla extract

400 g/14 oz plain flour

1 tsp bicarbonate of soda

½ tsp freshly grated nutmeg

pinch of salt

55 g/2 oz pecan nuts, finely
    chopped

Cinnamon coating

1 tbsp caster sugar

2 tbsp ground cinnamon

Put the butter and sugar into a bowl and mix well with a wooden spoon, then beat in the eggs and vanilla extract. Sift in the flour, bicarbonate of soda, nutmeg and salt, add the pecan nuts and stir until thoroughly combined. Shape the dough into a ball, wrap in clingfilm and chill in the refrigerator for 30–60 minutes.

Preheat the oven to 190°C/375°F/Gas Mark 5. Line two baking sheets with baking paper.

For the cinnamon coating, mix together the caster sugar and cinnamon in a shallow dish. Scoop up tablespoons of the cookie dough and roll into balls. Roll each ball in the cinnamon mixture to coat and place on the prepared baking sheets, spaced well apart.

Bake in the preheated oven for 10–12 minutes, until golden brown. Leave to cool for 5–10 minutes, then transfer to wire racks to cool completely.

Jam Sandwich Cookies

Makes 24

225 g/8 oz unsalted butter, softened

100 g/3½ oz caster sugar

200 g/7 oz plain flour, plus extra for dusting

pinch of salt

100 g/3½ oz ground almonds

55 g/2 oz raspberry jam

55 g/2 oz apricot jam

2 tbsp icing sugar

Cream together the butter and sugar until pale and fluffy. Add the flour, salt and ground almonds and stir until thoroughly combined. Shape the dough into a ball, wrap in clingfilm and chill in the refrigerator for 2 hours.

Preheat the oven to 150°C/300°F/Gas Mark 2. Roll out the dough out on a lightly floured surface to about 5 mm/¼ inch thick. Stamp out cookies with a 7-cm/2¾-inch plain round cutter. Use a small round cutter to stamp out the centre from half the cookies and put the cookies on two large non-stick baking sheets.

Bake in the preheated oven for 25–30 minutes, or until golden. Leave to cool for 5–10 minutes, then transfer to wire racks to cool completely.

Spoon the raspberry jam onto half the whole cookies. Spoon the apricot jam onto the remaining whole cookies. Top with the cookie rings, pressing down gently, and sift the icing sugar over the tops.